PANIC DISORDER WORKBOOK

THE END OF PANIC ATTACKS

Self-Therapeutic Solutions To Let Your Anxiety and Worry Fade Away For Good

CHARLEE HUBER

Table of Contents

PART I

Chapter 1:

Understanding Panic Attacks and Panic Disorders

Imagine the fear of watching a giant wave coming roaring towards you, while you stand frozen, unable to move an inch.

It is frightening. Have you ever experienced any such fear?
Imagine having extreme breathing difficulty all of a sudden, like having an asthma attack, without suffering from asthma.

It's scary and suffocating. Have you been in any such situation ever?
Imagine being in a situation when you are quite sure that you are not going to survive that crisis; only there is no such crisis.

It is a terrible experience. Have you been through it?
These are real-life situations that a panic attack might look like. To an onlooker, a panic may look like an overreaction. Most people consider panic attacks as dodging tactics using which you can escape facing tough situations. However, they are unable to understand that during a panic attack, the victim experiences difficulty in breathing, the actual feeling of an allergic reaction is there.

For many victims, there is a feeling of the throat closing up, feels like throat tightening, and it seems like a reaction of a body as if you were about to die, nausea, heart palpitation, excessive sweating, blackouts, chest pain, and complete loss of control are some of the common symptoms panic attack victims may experience during the attacks.

Panic attacks can come out of the blue without a prior warning or even without triggers. They are scarier than they sound because the panic attack victim can feel them approaching because there's nowhere to run. The warning signal is coming from the inside, and you can't run away from yourself.

Many people start saying breathe deeply, relax, or be calm, but all these suggestions are useless because the words don't reach the effective areas. Deep breathing can help the victim relax and avoid panic attacks, but that advice and assurance must come from inside. The realization that you can avert the attack by simply diverting your mind and staying calm must be there in you. There is no doubt that a panic attack victim would have to work on developing this confidence and realization, but it is very much possible.

What Is a Panic Attack?

Excessive anxieties and fears can lead to panic attacks. During a panic attack, the victim can experience several symptoms like racing heart, heart palpitation, excessive shaking, breathing difficulties, and nausea. Things simply start slipping out of control, and the victim starts feeling very helpless and vulnerable. Every panic attack victim doesn't experience all the symptoms mentioned above. As per the Diagnostic and Statistical Manual of Mental Disorders, fourth edition, if a victim experiences any of the four symptoms from the list given below, the victim is considered to have experienced a panic attack.

The real tell-tale sign of a panic attack is that it builds up rapidly. A person could be doing fine just a few minutes ago, and all of a sudden can start exhibiting signs of fear, anxiety, pain, and discomfort. A panic attack generally reaches its peak within ten minutes of the beginning.

Important Symptoms, the Victim of a Panic Attack, Is Likely to Experience:

(A person experiencing at least four of the symptoms at the same time is classified as experiencing a panic attack.)

1. Sensations of shortness of breath or smothering
2. Palpitations, pounding heart, or accelerated rate of heart
3. Trembling or shaking
4. Feeling lightheaded, unsteady, dizzy, or faint
5. Fear of losing control or going crazy
6. Chills or hot flushes
7. Sweating
8. Feeling of choking
9. Discomfort or chest pain
10. Nausea or abdominal distress
11. Fear of dying
12. Paresthesias (tingling sensations or numbness)
13. Derealization (a sense of unreality) or depersonalization (feeling detached from oneself)

As mentioned above, panic attacks symptoms appear very fast and do not allow the victim to understand much. It can peak within a short span of just 10 minutes, and hence initially, the victims generally do not get a chance to react properly.

A panic attack can make the victim feel like he/she isn't going to survive it. To some, the acute chest pain looks like a heart attack, and to others, the breathing difficulty episodes brought by panic attacks resemble asthma attacks. Most victims end up in emergency rooms only to be told later on that they had a panic attack.

It is important to understand that panic attacks don't last very long. A panic attack can begin out of the blue without a trigger and may reach its peak within 10 minutes. However, in most cases, panic attacks get resolved within half an hour. It is rare for a panic attack to last an hour.

Although panic attacks may last only for half an hour, for the victim, this duration may seem like an eternity. The whole period is physically and emotionally very stressful and overwhelming. It is the extreme stress experienced during the panic attack that may make it feel like a very long period, and it can be emotionally churning.

It is very important to note that there is no specific cause of panic attacks. Panic attacks can be caused by various stressors, and the genetic buildup of a person can make a person prone to panic attacks. However, people with mood disorders and long-standing anxiety issues are naturally soft-targets of panic attacks. Severe stress, major transitions in life, a feeling of acute vulnerability, and several medical conditions can also make a person prone to panic attacks.

What Is Panic Disorder and Should You Be Worried About It?

Panic disorder is having an extended fear of panic attacks all the time, even when you haven't had a panic attack in a month or more.

It is very much possible for a person to just have one or two episodes of panic attacks and then never have them ever. You were passing through a bad patch in life that made you insecure and vulnerable and caused a panic attack. When then phase passes away, you might not experience a panic attack ever again. Unfortunately, some people experience repeated panic attacks, and they undergo substantial behavioral changes making anxiety a part of their lives. They are always anxious about the next attack to come. Such people can be termed as suffering from **Panic Disorder**.

Symptoms That a Person Might be Developing Panic Disorder are:

- Constant worry about panic attacks
- Frequent episodes of panic attacks out of the blue
- Clear avoidance of things and situations that might have led to a panic attack

Panic disorders are the quiet periods between panic attacks, and they can be more harmful than panic attacks as they can severely affect the life and functioning of the victim. They can be as threatening as the silence before a storm, and that's what keeps the victims on edge.

Emotionally, panic disorder can take a toll on the mental health of the victim as it keeps the mind full of fearful thoughts and anxieties. Finding a diversion can get difficult in such a condition. The victims are unable to push the fear of an attack from their mind, and they are always in fear of an impending attack.

Chapter 2:

Anxiety and Panic Attacks Aren't the Same

There are many common symptoms in anxiety and panic attacks, and that makes people draw a misleading conclusion that having anxiety disorders and panic attacks or panic disorders is all the same.

Very Important

You must make it very clear in your mind that having a panic attack is an easily treatable condition. If you've just had a few episodes of panic attacks, you can just go to a doctor and get treatment for that. A simple medication routine of a fortnight can help you get over panic attacks. However, treatment of anxiety disorders is a very lengthy process that may take years while using both medication and therapy.

Therefore, if you or someone you know just had a panic attack, there is no reason to worry as it is a treatable condition.

Differentiating between both the conditions can be a bit tricky and may need professional help.

However, here are some broad points that can help you understand the difference:

- Anxieties are generally very specific. There are triggers for anxiety. You know the things that can make you feel anxious. There would be specific stressors and triggers that can trigger anxiety in you. On the other hand, panic attacks usually come without a trigger.

- A big difference between anxiety and panic is the way you feel them. Panic attacks are sudden and intense. A panic attack can start all of a sudden without a trigger and would reach its peak in a short span of 10 minutes. Although they are fast and intense and the entire duration of a panic attack may seem like an eternity, usually they don't last longer than half an hour and would rarely extend for an hour. Whereas anxiety can keep building for months.

- Initially, the anxiety would be less, and it can keep intensifying over a long period. As time passes, your anxiety would keep getting stronger, and it simply doesn't pass away like a panic attack.

- Anxieties are usually followed by a long period of worries. It keeps the mind occupied and leads to overthinking and development of deep fear. Panic attacks end fast, and you will feel all the pressure and fear melting away. You'd feel the intense weight being lifted from your head.

Generalized anxiety in this way is much more dangerous and complex than sporadic episodes of panic attacks. It can last for anywhere between a few minutes to your whole lifetime.

However, every fear and anxiety is not bad. Generally, we feel anxious about things we are not comfortable with. When we are anxious, there can be a rapid pounding of heart, increased pulse, sweating, and tension. You get a general feeling of your inability to cope with a certain situation, and hence defensive mechanism gets activated. Most of the time, people choose to avoid things and situations that may cause anxieties. But, that's not possible in the case of panic attacks as they can come without any such trigger or stressor.

Anxiety disorders should never be ignored as they form the basis of several complicated conditions like social anxiety disorder (SAD), obsessive-compulsive disorder (OCD), posttraumatic stress disorder (PTSD), generalized anxiety disorder (GAD), etc.

Chapter 3: Biological and Psychological Causes of Panic Attacks

Biological Causes of Panic Attacks

There is a lot about the brain and its functioning that modern medical science is yet to discover. We know a lot of things, and we are still in the process of finding out a lot more things. The exact physiological causes of panic attacks are also among the few things medical science is trying to find more about.

The science known until now strongly suggests that panic attacks are caused by the faulty alarm system in our brain.

There is an area in the brain known as Locus Ceruleus. This region has a high concentration of adrenaline-like neurons. The impulse conductors of the nerve cells connect this part to:

- The cerebral cortex (the part of the brain determining intelligence, personality, motor function, senses, etc.)
- The limbic system (responsible for our emotions and higher mental function)
- Thalamus (part of the brain managing pain and emotions)
- Hypothalamus (controls the nervous system and hormone signals)

Effectively, any activity in this part of the brain is going to affect your overall functionality.

This locus ceruleus region and the adrenaline-like neurons can stimulate your body to release hormones that can activate a severe 'fight or flight response.' The body needs this hormone when it is in any kind of danger.

When in danger, the body pumps in adrenaline or epinephrine can make you feel very frightened. In a real-life dangerous situation, that the glucose supply to the cells would be stopped, and all the glucose in the bloodstream would be made available to generate maximum thrust for any action. This simply means that when you are in some grave danger, the power and thrust available to get out of that danger goes up considerably.

This of a scenario where you come face to face with a wild animal. The animal is a quadruped, and hence it has a higher speed than you. In a normal situation, there is no chance for you to outrun that animal. However, due to a very high adrenaline rush in your blood and the resulting fight or flight response, you'll be able to run much faster than your normal capacity to manage survival. This rush is shortlived. It is not possible to manage that speed in normal circumstances, but our body makes a desperate attempt to survive.

This system is there to amplify the chances of survival in dangerous circumstances. Our ancestors had to survive in the wild with no claws, horns, or brute force, whereas the animals were faster, more powerful, and had the accessories like claws, big teeth, and horns. That could make survival difficult, and hence this system was very helpful.

The alarm bells in the locus ceruleus region activate the adrenaline-like neurons, which cause a noradrenergic overload. This is a helpful process in threatening situations. However, in the case of a panic attack, this process gets activated without any stressor or danger trigger. Not only this alarm system gets activated falsely, but it is also very severe in response sending the victim in a state of panic.

Available knowledge and data suggest that this alarm system in our brains is prone to malfunction. Like any alarm system, one or two episodes can occur and then never happen again. This is a reason some people may experience panic attacks once or twice in their lives, never to experience them ever again. Even if you get a panic attack, there is nothing to worry about as just the alarm system has gone off, and otherwise, there is no threat to the body in general. This is a reason panic attacks require no hospitalization or medical care. As there is little understanding of the system, all the causes of the malfunction are not clear, but data shows that hereditary predisposition can make a person prone to such attacks.

There is a high probability that you might have heard the term serotonin. It is commonly used in connection with the things that bring a calming effect to the mind. Instantly after your body has had passed through a severe crisis, you'd notice a feeling of complete relaxation. This feeling of complete relaxation, calm, and peace is brought upon by the effect of serotonin. It is a neuromodulator that helps in modulating anxiety. Gamma-aminobutyric Acid (GABA) is also a neuromodulator chemical. Through several studies, scientists have concluded that when there is a chemical imbalance in the brain, causing low levels of GABA and serotonin, it can lead to panic attacks.

Most theories suggest that the physiological cause of a panic attack somewhere lies in the chemical imbalance in the brain and the faulty alarm system that evokes a crisis response. However, the good thing in these studies is that they suggest this fact with clarity that although the alarm system might be faulty, there is no problem with the basic functioning of the mind and the body.

This means that panic attacks are not a danger for the body. Hence, you don't need to rush to the emergency room every time you have a panic attack or something similar to that. If you could just relax and stay calm, the surge of emotions being experienced by you would pass without an incident.

However, this is easier said than done. The kind of crisis a panic victim feels is only known to that victim. The fear is debilitating. It reduces the victim to nothing. It tears down the personality of the victim. The victims may also face social humiliation due to their sudden reactions. There is no way a panic attack victim can choose the place and time of a panic attack, and that is a reason most victims develop a fear of being in public.

Psychological Causes of Panic Attacks

Panic attacks are strong fear signals being generated in your brain, and your thinking can have a major role to play in that. The kind of temperament you have, the kind of people you socialize with, the kind of job you do, the state of your financial security, etc. are some of the things that can also have a major role in a panic attack.

If any of these things are leading to any kind of insecurity, you can be at risk of a panic attack. You must remember that any kind of major stress in life can lead to a panic attack, and hence leading a balanced life is important.

If you are a person who is sensitive to negative emotions or who cannot handle stressful events, you must work on this aspect of life along with someone who is encouraging and supporting. Fear of things that are very stressful for you can also lead to panic attacks.

Major life events like the demise of a loved one, childhood experience of physical or sexual abuse, or any other such traumatic event recently can also lead to panic attacks.

Abuse of drugs and alcohol can also lead to panic abuse.

Chapter 4: Who Is At a Greater Risk of Panic Attacks?

Anyone can have panic attacks. This is a problem that can strike anyone. Even the marines, who are fitter than the fittest, can suffer from panic attacks. Therefore, if you are fortunate enough to not have experienced any, all you can do is remain cautious. You must remember that even if a panic attack comes, it is a treatable condition.

However, if you fall under any of these categories, you should remain more cautious:

- **Women:** Unfortunately, women have twice the risk of having a panic attack as compared to men. If you are a woman with claustrophobia or any other anxiety disorder, then also your risk of having a panic attack is very high. You'll need to be extra cautious about the things that can cause severe stress.

- **People between 20-29 Age Group:** Although panic attacks can come in any age group, people in the age group of 20-29 years are more likely to experience panic attacks. However, that doesn't mean that people in the younger or older age groups are immune. It can strike at any age.

- **People with a Family History:** As we have already discussed it, if you have someone in your close family with a history of panic attacks or other mental conditions, your risk of having panic attacks can go up.

- **Stressful Life-events:** If you've been through some very stressful life events such as job loss, failure in any big competition, rejection in something crucial, marriage or divorce, or history of abuse, then also the risk of a panic attack will increase.

- **Anxious or Overthinking Attitude:** Some people have anxiety in their attitude. They are never able to feel safe. They always have a lingering fear that something might go wrong. This feeling is even more overpowering when they are sitting at some very pleasant and secure place. It is their mind at play, all the time. Such people are naturally predisposed to panic attacks.

- **Mental Health Illnesses:** If a person has been struggling with generalized anxiety disorder or depression, then the risk of panic attacks will increase.

- **History of Substance Abuse:** Any person with a history of substance abuse will be at a higher risk of panic attacks. Alcohol disorders will also increase the risk many times over.

Chapter 5: Tips to Cope With Panic Attacks When They Strike

You must accept the fact that panic attacks can come. The biggest problem with panic attack victims is that they can't come to terms with the fact that they have panic attacks.

You must realize that you've had a panic attack, and it's okay to have one. You are not the first one and for sure not the last one to have one. Therefore, the best thing to do is to be calm as it is just a phase, and it'd pass away.

Many a time, when someone has a panic attack, the people standing around ask the victim to breathe deeply or be calm and that never really works. It doesn't mean that deep breathing or staying calm are not effective techniques. The victim is simply not in a condition to hear or understand these things. The power to comprehend things said by others during a panic attack goes down. But, if you train your mind and understand the power of deep breathing and other relaxation techniques, you can effectively avoid panic attacks or minimize their severity.

We'll deal with two things in this chapter:

1. Ways to Prevent Panic Attacks
2. Ways to Cope with Panic Attacks

- **Practice Breathing Exercises:** This is probably one of the most important advice you'll ever hear in panic attack prevention. When having a panic attack, the biggest problem faced is breathlessness. The brain starts getting devoid of oxygen. If you practice deep breathing exercises, you'll be able to prevent panic attacks to a great extent. Breathing exercises are very easy and won't take longer than a few minutes of your time daily. You can practice yoga asanas as they are especially very helpful in preventing panic attacks.

- **Light Exercises:** Exercise has a very positive impact on the brain. When you exercise, the body releases hormones called endorphins that help you in relaxing and also induce a happy mood. Regular exercise can promote a sense of positivity in you and help in preventing panic attacks. However, you must remember that this usually helps when you do light exercises. When you are doing strength training and other accelerated stuff, you must be careful when you are hyperventilating as it can trigger a panic attack. In such a circumstance, your priority must remain to catch your breath first.

- **Manage Blood Sugar Levels:** Keeping your blood sugar levels managed is also a way to prevent panic attacks.

- **Avoid Stimulants like Caffeine, Nicotine, and Alcohol:** Most people know that drug abuse can lead to panic abuse, but a large number of people find it hard to believe that excessive amounts of caffeine, nicotine, and alcohol can also trigger panic attacks. You must try to avoid these.

- **Cognitive Behavioral Therapy (CBT):** This therapy can help you identify and change negative thought patterns leading to panic attacks.

Ways to Cope With Panic Attacks

- **Accept and Recognize:** Panic attacks are short, and they are harmless. You must realize the fact that the episodes you experience don't last long. No matter how bad you might feel at that moment, panic attacks pass, and you are safe again. Therefore, there is no need to fear panic attacks or to stay in denial. If you are having a panic attack, you must recognize it. Once you learn to recognize and accept the fact that you are having a panic attack, it'd be easier to understand that they will pass safely.

- **Deep Breathing:** Breathing deeply while you are having a panic attack is always helpful. Shortness of breath or breathing difficulties are common symptoms of panic attacks, and hence deep breathing will not only help in getting over the panic attacks, but it might even prevent a full-blown panic attack even from happening.

- **Inhale Lavender:** Lavender is a stimulant that can help you feel relaxed. If you get panic attacks frequently, you can keep lavender with you and smell a bit of it when having an attack, and it can help you feel relaxed faster.

- **Medication:** Some medications can help you in coping with panic attacks. If you are having panic attacks frequently, you must consult a doctor and take medication for it.

- **Avoid External Stimuli:** Many a time, loud noise in the background, bright lights, or any other kind of stimuli can also accelerate a panic attack. If you feel a panic attack coming, try to find a peaceful place as it can help you focus inwards, and you'll be able to cope with the panic attack better.

- **Try Meditation Techniques:** Meditation is a great way to train your mind to remain peaceful and calm. It is an effective technique to make your mind avoid fearful thoughts or to divert attention from them. If you can practice meditation for a few minutes daily, you'll be able to overcome the problem of panic attacks to a great extent. There are several meditation forms and techniques that you can try. Some of the effective ones are given below:

  o **Mindfulness Meditation:** Most of our panic attacks are either fuelled by our memories of the past or the fears of the future. We are seldom scared of the present as we rarely live in the present. This meditation technique can help you train your mind to live in the present or live mindfully. It can become an effective tool to cope with panic attacks.

  o **Diversion of Mind:** During panic attacks, the mind gets focused on a negative thought. If you can focus your attention on a physical point in front of you and meditate only on that point bringing your complete awareness on it, you will be able to prevent or get over the panic attack faster as your mind will get diverted.

  o **Muscle Relaxing:** Stiffening of muscles and sensation of pain can also act as a trigger for a panic attack. Practicing progressive-muscle relaxation meditation can help you in relaxing the whole body, and it also takes away the mind from fearful thoughts.

o **Picture a Happy Place:** Guided meditation using imagery of a happy place that you can imagine will also help you in coping better from panic attacks. When your mind is thinking about a happy place, it is very relaxed and calm.

o **Use Positive Affirmation:** You can use positive affirmations during a panic attack to reassure yourself that the panic attack will pass shortly without any incident. Positive affirmations like, 'this is a phase, it'll pass,' or 'you are doing fine, there is nothing to worry' can help you in dealing with the panic attacks better.

Chapter 6: The 8-week Plan to Deal With Panic Attacks

Fighting your fears can be a life-long journey. The fears are not physical; they reside in our minds. The more we think about them, the more intense they get. This chapter would help you understand the ways to tackle the things that have been scaring you for all these years.

The plan has been divided into 8 weeks. 1 week for each plan. During that week, you'll have to work only on that specific issue. You may not be addressing the whole problem, but it'll help you in dealing with the issue in the end.

You must understand that the psychology of fear can be ingrained deep inside your mind, and hence it may take you much longer than 8 weeks too. However, no matter how long it takes, if you follow these 8 steps, you'll be able to get the fear of panic attacks due to specific stressors out of your mind.

Week 1

Identify the Triggers, Fears, and Problematic Behavior

When dealing with any kind of problem, it is very important to understand that problem clearly. The biggest problem with panic attacks lies in the fact that you do not know the things causing them. However, that doesn't mean that you are completely oblivious to your fears. Your panic attack is just a sum-total of your fears. If you can identify and address your fears correctly, you'll be able to get rid of them.

Our fears are not random. They originate from various sections of our lives. We may have a fear of things related to work, education, social interaction, or any specific part of these. Once you identify those fears or triggers, dealing with them would be considerably easy. During the first week, you need to analyze every area in your life and note down the things that may be causing stress, fear, or panic. You should be as detailed as possible in this.

Main Areas of Concern:

Work-Related: Most people feel stressed at work. Although that may not cause a panic attack in every individual, there can be some people who might feel highly stressed at their workplace. You should think of all the things at the workplace that make you feel stressed. Try to be very specific. Like if you feel a sense of panic while being called to give a presentation, you must note it down.

Social Interaction: This is another area where many people feel highly insecure. Some people have anxieties about social interaction, and it can cause a panic attack. You must evaluate if social interactions invoke such a reaction in you. Try to be very specific and focused here. Think of the things that might make you feel nervous. Like if being called to sign in a function makes you feel anxious. Most people will feel nervous in that situation, but do you feel a fight or flight response kicking in?

Health and Well-being: People can get anxious thinking about their health or the health of a family member. Think if you have any fear related to that.

Relationship: Think of your fears related to your existing or past relationships and if they are making you feel anxious.

Other Factors: Think of any other fear that might be lingering deep inside you. There can be many other kinds of fears in mind. Some people are afraid of snakes and scorpions; others are scared of allergies; some are scared of heights. Think of the issue that keeps lingering in your mind.

PinPoint the Issue: You must single out the issue. When you have the problem in view, it is always easy to deal with it. Do not try to limit your entry to any specific thing. List all your fears. Try to know everything that has the potential to make you feel anxious or bring a panic attack.

Week 2

Identify Your Negative Thought Patterns

Once you have the list of things that make you fearful, you can move ahead to deal with the thoughts that lead to such fears. The fears do not come from outside. They are an exaggeration of the thoughts we have about them. Some people may faint when asked to give a speech in front of a gathering while others feel themselves at ease doing so. The task was the same for both, but their minds were working in different ways. The fearful mind started thinking about the consequences of giving that speech like being ridiculed, laughed at, talked about behind the back, saying something unreasonable, etc. The fearless mind saw an opportunity to gain popularity and express views. The situation was the same, but different minds made different assumptions and conclusions. You need to keep in mind that the assumptions made by both could have been wrong. The fearless speakers may have got booed; it happens all the time. However, the fearful speakers would have never reached the podium of completed the speech because the presumptions were incorrect, to begin with.

Our fears are caused by our thoughts, and hence it is important to identify negative thought patterns in the mind to deal with those fears.

Negative thought patterns can be classified in the following broader terms:

Unhelpful Thoughts: These are the thoughts that lead to doubts as you start thinking anything. If you are thinking of undertaking a journey, they'll lead you to think about accidents or bad things that may happen on the journey. If you are thinking of applying for a job, these thoughts will make you think about getting rejected and make you experience that feeling. You must identify if you have unhelpful thoughts very often.

What if Thoughts: These are the thoughts that try to analyze every situation. It may seem logical to think of all the sides of the coin, but it isn't as simple as that. These thoughts will lead you to emphasize on the negative outcomes.

Critical Thoughts: These are the thoughts that make you look at the negative side of everything. You become critical of your abilities, and this can start making you feel insecure, leading to panic attacks.

Victimizing Thoughts: These are the thoughts that make you feel like a victim in every situation. The victim mentality can be very dangerous as it kills all kinds of initiative. It makes you feel exploited and vulnerable, and it can lead to panic attacks. You must identify if you have victimizing thoughts.

Know the Way You Think: To solve any problem, you must know the problem first. Your thoughts are the fuel that leads to the rocket of fear that takes you on panic trips. If you want to avoid panic attacks, it is pertinent that you identify your thought pattern. You must know the way your brain thinks, and then only you will be able to make a strategy to break that thought pattern.

Week 3 and 4

Dissociate From the Negative Thought Patterns

Once the task of identifying negative thought patterns has been completed, you need to devise strategies to change those thought patterns. This may take even longer than two weeks.

Thought patterns develop over a very long period. You may have been practicing the same thought pattern since your childhood. Most thought patterns are picked from the surrounding. This solid conditioning makes the breaking of thought patterns a tough and time-consuming task as you'd need a lot of practice.

However, the only way to do this is to practice it over and over again to make this thought pattern a habit.

Practice Labeling Your Thoughts: This is the first thing that you must do. You learn to label the thought. When you have a negative thought in your mind, learn to label it as 'just a thought.' Our mind is conditioned to consider such thoughts as facts since once it is considered a fact, it is easy to believe. You'll have to identify every negative thought and label it as just a thought, and then it'd be easier to work with it. It wouldn't ring in your brain as the gospel truth.

Make It Funny: If there is any such thought that is making you feel insecure, or which is intimidating you, try to say that out in a funny tone. This simple exercise would help you make light of it. That thought wouldn't remain very fearful or intimidating.

Push Positive Thinking to that Thought: Most negative thoughts become powerful because they never get countered by a positive thought. Try countering the negative thought in your mind with a positive idea.

Evaluate that Thought: You must grade every thought as helpful or unhelpful and discard unhelpful ideas. Once you start grading your thoughts, it'd be easier for you to distance yourself from negative thoughts. They wouldn't have command over your mind.

Find time in the future to ponder over it: If any specific thought is still lingering in your mind, find a time in the future to think it over and get it out of the way. Breaking negative thought patterns should be your focus. If there is any thought that's causing trouble in your mind, either counter it positively or get it out of the mind for the time being.

Week 5

Facing the Fears Head-on

Fear is our biggest enemy. Once you have broken the negative thought pattern, your mind will be able to think about things in a much better way. Yet, it may not be ready to shun all fears. If you are faced with situations that filled you with a sense of anxiety previously, they'll have the same impact again. The correct way to face fears is to experience and overcome them. However, this can't be done without preparation.

> **Facing Fears in a Safe Environment:** The best way to move in this direction is to face your fears in a safe environment. If you feel that you have an intense fear of public speaking, begin by speaking only in front of a small group of your friends. When you see that you have a familiar group of faces that is even encouraging you, it'll be easier to give your first speech. Give a few speeches like than and then begin expanding the circle. Include a few people who are friends of friends and then strangers. When you move in a step-by-step manner in a safe environment conquering any fear becomes possible. The key is not to expose yourself to the fearful situation all at once but to do that gradually.

Week 6

Practice Relaxation

Completely relaxing the mind is the key to overcoming panic attacks, but this is just not a psychological process as there is biology involved too. As we have discussed, panic attacks can have some severe symptoms like shortness of breath, nausea, chest pain, etc. All these symptoms emerge because your body has a quick and severe response to a stressor. You must learn to keep the body relaxed to manage panic attacks successfully.

These relaxation techniques can help you in dealing with panic attacks is an amazing way. Not only will you feel more relaxed, but even the recovery from a panic attack would be very much easier.

Practice Relaxation Meditation: Relaxation meditation is the best when it comes to panic relief or relieving stress. It is easy and simple. You can practice it sitting or lying down as you feel comfortable. Just close your eyes and keep your awareness focused on a point. Keep breathing deeply and just push any thought that comes to mind. Your awareness should just focus on the point you are looking at with your eyes closed. Make everything else less important than this. This simple meditation will help you achieve a state of thoughtlessness.

Deep Breathing: This is one of the most important exercises in dealing with panic attacks or any other kind of anxiety. It is very simple and highly effective. You can follow it anywhere anytime. Whenever you feel a panic attack coming, you can start focusing on your breath and begin deep breathing. You'll see that a majority of times, you'll just not have a panic attack. Deep breathing is as simple as its name. Keep taking deep breaths in and then release your breath very slowly. You should also practice it at least once a day.

Progressive Muscle Relaxation: Stiffness of muscles is another cause of panic attacks. The pain and stiffness in the body keep getting ignored and emerges as a negative impulse. An easy way to get rid of that is to follow progressive muscle relaxation techniques. In this meditation technique, you scan your whole body through your awareness and release the pressure and anxiety built up in those areas.

It gives you effective control of your body and also fills you up with a realization that there is no stress or anxiety inside you.

Meditation Using Guided Imagery: This is the best way to manage panic attacks. You can have a recorded guided meditation session using positive imagery liked by you. You'll be free to choose a location or situation of your choice. You can record it yourself or get a pre-recorded one. Whenever you fear a panic attack, you can switch on that guided meditation session, and the recollection of that happy place can help you avoid the negative thoughts that may lead to a panic attack.

Week 7

Practice Mindfulness

This week, you must practice mindfulness. Most people confuse meditation and mindfulness as being interchangeable terms, but they are not. Meditation is the art of looking inside. You don't run away from thoughts, you look inside the thoughts and try to understand them objectively. Mindfulness, on the other hand, is the practice of doing things mindfully. You stop running in an automated mode and start putting your consciousness behind every action you take.

For instance, when you eat, you pay attention to all the aspects of the food. You feel the taste, the aroma, the flavors, and the texture of the food. You pay attention to the process of eating. You chew the food properly and feel it while you chew. This process not only improves your understanding of every process, but it also helps in eliminating any kind of fear present in your mind regarding them.

Some Parts of Mindfulness Practice are:

Meditation: Be meditative in everything you do. Stop doing things in an automated mode. Take cognizance of every action you take.

Be Observant: Observe things more carefully and closely. Don't allow things to pass in front of you like that. Be observant of the things around you.

Stop Before Reacting: Before you react to anything, stop for a moment and think about that thing, the reaction it requires, and the kind of reaction you were going to give.

Learn to Shift Awareness: Learn the art of shifting your awareness on the object of your choice. For instance, if you are having fearful things about your flight, you should be able to fix your awareness at the swiftly moving second hand of your clock or any other such thing.

Week 8

Getting the Experience

This is the week to experience and practice all that you have learned in the past two months. The process may take a bit longer than two months in your case, but there is no need to worry as this is not to scale.

Just go out in the world and face your fear head-on.

However, you must observe the things you have been able to incorporate easily and the things that still need some work.

PART II

Chapter 1: Anxiety, The Monster Within

"I know what it's like to be afraid of your own mind."

- Dr. Reid from Criminal Minds

- Obsessing over small worries that constantly distract you
- Whirling from action to action to try to quiet your minds' nagging
- Attempting to drown out anxious thoughts in any way possible, solemnly wishing they would just disappear

If you are here with us today, you are likely living through all the above and more, trying strategy after strategy to eliminate these causes of stress. Or, perhaps you are seeking help for a loved one that has anxiety that is weighing them down. Or, maybe you are simply here to feed your curiosity of what anxiety is and how it plagues the mind. No matter, I work with anxiety every day and have spent the majority of my existence on Earth immersed in it.

My grandfather was such a worrier that he physically shook, *constantly*. His body would tremble from the overwhelming magnitude of worry that lurked within him. He was a burly southern man who favored anything outdoors and fishing. His long, curly locks framed his rounded face with an always generous smile. When he was at his warmest, he was a magnet to others. However, his most natural state was when he was in worry mode.

What did he worry about? Anything and everything. He was worried about all the typical things that grandparents do; along with I'm sure many countless unspoken things.

"Do you have enough to eat?"

"Do you need the salt or pepper?"

"Are you comfortable? Too hot? Too cold?"

Even though he was a burly man, his voice was soft, so anyone listening had to lean in. I think he like the intimacy it afforded. Whenever we were all at ease, he was at ease.

Us grandkids always ran with the joke, *"Grampy, can we pass you the salt and pepper?"* His anxiousness would disappear with a smile and flush of embarrassment. We did this to show our appreciation, to relieve the tension and let him know he was never a burden and that we loved our big burly gramps for who he was.

Our gramps was a people-person, always curious and invested in others. I have very clear memories of coming home and hearing his low but small voice in the answering machine, *"Hello, it is just me again. Just checking in to see how you are coming along..."*

He needed that regular assurance that everything was, in fact, alright and always preferred to hear it firsthand. And if he could do things for someone, that was even better.

As Gramps aged, his anxiety escalated and he became less able to use it in a constructive manner. There were less and fewer ways for him to release his anxious feelings, to the point he became crippled with worried on a daily basis. When I search into where my own anxiety stemmed from, a picture of Grampy always pops into my mind. When I studied anxiety in graduate school, his shaking body was a perfect analogy. The more time I spent exposed to the study of anxiety in the human body, I began to understand my grandfather better than he likely understood himself most days. I also realized how persuasive anxiety was throughout our family's history. It was what set the foundation for me to deeply understand how much anxiety affected emotions and behaviors.

Thankfully, no one else in my family shook as much as my grandfather did from anxiety; however, looking back, anxiety was the hub of all the spectrum of extremes my family endured. My mother was motivated by her anxiety, while my father was like a balloon, letting stress and anxious feelings build up until he popped with rage.

While no one in my immediate family was ever diagnosed with an anxiety disorder, I can still imagine that just like so many others, they would have felt the same shameful stigma that comes along with all mental health problems, thinking that something is wrong with them. They were simply noticing things in their lives and felt deeply about them; they just didn't have the tools and knowledge to cope with the overload of information.

Through my years as a psychologist, I have gained a different perspective on anxiety and how it alters thoughts and feelings. I have come to see anxiety as a resource and seek to embrace its value in our everyday lives.

Anxiety derives from the feeling of realizing that something we genuinely care about may be at risk, as well as the arrival of resources that we need in order to protect it. Anxiety prompts us to look closer and pay better attention to messages we receive and helps us to gain the motivation we need to take control of situations. The key to getting back a life driven by anxiety and fear is to take control. This is where I have used my knowledge to help others, in ultimately steering them in a different direction of gaining back their willpower.

How Anxiety Overshadows Everyday Lives

Living in denial, second-guessing your every move, thinking ill thoughts about your future, living in fear of the unknown; all these things can overshadow a person's life and lead to constant anxiety.

If you or a loved one is plagued by anxiety, you have probably endured panic attacks and constant negative nagging in your head on a regular basis or have a phobia of some kind feel ashamed of their "sickness."

Anxiety has the power to make everyday folks feel insane, even though they truly aren't. Just like with all people, some days are better than others, but those who experience symptoms caused by these mental ailments typically have a higher count of bad than good days.

46

They often feel that they are always under a dark cloud that pours rain, but that rain is not made up of just water. Those drops from the sky above their head are created from startling visions, disturbing logic, feelings of worthlessness and/or hopelessness and looks that they receive from both loved ones and strangers when they truly believe they are in a type of personal crisis or feel as if they are about to be pushed over the edge. This is just a small portion of what it is like to live with anxiety.

What is Anxiety?

Anxiety, in its simplest form, is a bodily reaction to unfamiliar or dangerous environments and scenarios. Everyone has the tendency to get anxious from time to time and feel distressed or uneasy. This happens perhaps before a big game, performing in front of an audience or right before a huge job interview. Feeling anxious is a natural response that our bodies can feel during moments like these. Anxiety gives us the boost we need to be consciously aware and alert to prepare us for certain situations.

Our body's "fight-or-flight" response is under this umbrella of reactions. But imagine feeling like this *all* the time, even during the calmest of moments?

Picture a life where you have issues concentrating on everyday tasks, where you may be frightened to leave the safety of your home when you cannot fall or stay asleep because your mind is in a constant whirlwind of thought? Living with an anxiety disorder is debilitating. That is putting it lightly in some cases.

Causes of Anxiety

Every one of us is unique, which means even common disorders, like anxiety and depression, resonate within each of us differently, as well as why we are living with anxiety, to begin with. There are several key factors that cause anxiety disorders to grow in the mind:

- Chemistry of the brain
- Environmental factors
- Genetics
- How we grew up
- Life events

The factors listed above are the basics that lay the groundwork to potentially be a victim of anxiety, but those below mixed with any of those above could set one up to be someone that is at a higher risk than others in the development of an anxiety disorder:

- Alcohol, prescription medication or drug abuse
- Chemical imbalances in the body and/or brain
- History of anxiety that runs in family bloodlines
- Occurrence of other mental health issues
- Physical, emotional or mental trauma
- Side effects one has on particular medications
- Stress that lasts an extended amount of time

The feelings and thoughts that anxiety promotes within a sufferer create a bubble that creates lonely thoughts and feelings, which is why it is no surprise that anxiety disorders are the most common of mental illnesses with the U.S, with **over 40 million American adults** living with one of these disorders as we speak.

If it is any consolation, you are by no means alone when it comes to feeling the way you do. There is still a lot of research being put into finding out why anxiety plagues so many individuals, its specific causes and why it resonates within individuals in such vast ways.

Signs & Symptoms of Anxiety Disorders

All of us will experience anxiety in our lives; it is a normal response to stressful life events. But as you have learned so far or experienced for yourself, these symptoms can become much larger than the events of stress them and can interfere heavily with a happy, healthy way of life.

Below are the most common symptoms of anxiety:

- **Worrying** that is disproportionate to the events that trigger it and is intrusive, making it challenging to concentrate on everyday tasks.
- **Agitation** that causes fast heartrates, sweaty hands, dry mouth, etc.
- **Restlessness** or feeling on edge with a constant uncomfortable urge to move that won't go away.
- Becoming **easily fatigued**, either in general or after a panic attack.
- **Difficulty focusing** on everyday tasks.
- **Issues retaining short-term memory** which results in a lack of performance in multiple areas of life.
- Becoming **easily irritable** in the day to day life.
- Constantly having **tense muscles** that may even heighten anxious feelings.
- **Issues falling and staying asleep** due to continued disturbances in the sleep cycle.
- **Panic attacks** that produce overwhelming sensations of fear.
- **Avoidance of social situations** due to a fear of being judged, humiliated, or embarrassed.
- **Extreme fears** about very specific situations or objects that are severe enough to interfere with normal functioning.

Understanding Social Anxiety

Imagine at random times, feeling so uncomfortable in particular situations to the point of not being able to process what is happening around you or difficulty breathing. Welcome to the life of those that deal with social anxiety. Social anxiety is classified by a major discomfort with social interactions as well as a fear of judgment. There are more than 15 million Americans that deal with this in their everyday lives that struggle with the awkwardness of social settings.

Symptoms of Social Anxiety

The main symptoms of this form of anxiety are feeling intensely anxious when in social situations or avoiding them altogether. Many sufferers have a constant feeling that 'something just isn't right', but are never able to pinpoint it.
As you can imagine, these people have a twisted way of thinking that includes false beliefs of situations and negative opinions from others. Many people fear the interaction days or weeks before the event, which means that social anxiety can manifest in other physical symptoms, such as:

- Sweating
- Shaking
- Diarrhea
- Upset stomach
- Muscle tension
- Blushing
- Confusion
- Pounding of heart
- Panic attacks

The key aspect of social anxiety to remember is that even though these folks have a fear of speaking or interacting with others, it doesn't mean they have nothing to say.

Below are things that those who suffer from social anxiety would say to others to help them understand how they feel:

"I do not want this and I cannot help it. It is not just a bit of nervousness that comes and goes. It is constant stress and living in a world that you start to not recognize."

"In my ability to speak right, I lack confidence. There are many times I want to say something, but hold back because I am afraid of how dumb it may sound or that I will be misunderstood. I am afraid of speaking in groups, phone calls, and approaching people the most.

"I am terrified of people's reactions when I do scrounge up the courage to finally speak."

"My anxiety socially is not a constant. There are certain situations that cause me more anxiety than others. It is a fluid disease."

"Many times, people don't realize that those with this anxiety disorder are suffering because of the lack of physical symptoms. Just because you cannot tell there is something wrong, doesn't mean there isn't."

"I cannot help how ridiculous it may seem."

"It hurts to know that people take my anxiety personally instead of just helping me out."

"I wish I had a social life, but my anxiety won't let me; I am not anti-social."

"It may look like I am zoning out from time to time, but I am actually practicing positive self-talk and breathing techniques to stay calm and ward off a panic attack."

"I am not trying to be standoffish, rude, or snobby, even though it may seem that way when I refuse hugs or don't wish to speak. I simply get overwhelmed and overstimulated easily. All I ask for is respect."

"I want people to break the ice and speak to me first. I am genuinely a nice person, I just have a fear I am unable to control."

"I wish more people understood that when I say I cannot come, it is because the situation I was invited to feels 'impossible', not because I don't feel like it."

"When I leave early, I am not being disrespectful. I just need to fight off a meltdown with some alone time."

"Social anxiety is not 'shyness'; that is like comparing a stab wound to a paper cut."
No one experiences social anxiety in the same way. Each day is like living a life of constant fear; worrying about the disapproval of others, rejection, not fitting in, etc. They are bound to be anxious to enter or begin a conversation.

Chapter 2: Acknowledging Your Anxiety

While the numbers of those that suffer from anxiety in the United States alone exceed 40 million, you may feel alone in your symptoms as well as what triggers them. Things that set off those anxious thoughts and feelings are a bit different for everyone who experiences anxiety. It is important to take time to focus on yourself and learn what things provide you with peace or create tension in your life.

Common Anxiety Triggers

- The hustle and bustle of everyday life. Life is always busy and there never seems to be time to slow down.
- The inevitable fact that we are only growing older.
- Driving, especially on freeways with many cars or across bridges.
- Not living up to the expectations that we set for ourselves.
- The sense of uncertainty. When we are not on control of situations we tend to freak out a bit. This comes from a lack of communication and anxiety making conclusions for us.
- Ambulance, fire or police sirens.
- Stresses at work – Not performing well enough, not having enough time during the course of the workday to get things done, etc.
- Simply thinking about what triggers your anxiety can be a cause for anxiousness in itself.
- Being too hot is often times directly associated with being claustrophobic.
- The inevitable part of life known as death. This especially goes for individuals who have experienced much loss in their lives.
- Being alone.

- The possibility of finding out that people do not like you as much as you think they do.
- Being judged or verbally attacked.
- Large crowds.
- The inability to predict the future. Those with anxiety often dislike surprises.
- Trying new things.
- Being far away from home or other places familiar to you.
- When many people speak to or at you all at once.
- The struggles that your children may face at school.
- Money! This is a big one. Whether it is saving for a big event such as a wedding or purchasing a home or car, the process of paying monthly bills while still trying to save money for other things.

Getting to the Root Causes of Your Anxiety

What many of us do not realize is that many causes that trigger our anxieties to flare up are actually self-produced. While you can blame your situation, family, friends, etc. for you distress, you are the one who perceives life as it goes on around you. The way you view it, analyze and take it all is all dependent on you. The root reasons behind the curtains of 'Play Anxiety' are usually caused by one of the following reasons.

Negative Self-Talk

It is said by research conducted by behavioral specialists that upwards of 77% of all the things we think to ourselves is quite counterproductive and negative. What we don't realize is that we are being our own worst critic and a detriment to ourselves. Learn to become consciously aware of the way you speak to yourself.

Write down any sort of negative thoughts for a day and then each day forward practice transforming those negative words or thoughts into a happy, loving one towards yourself. While it may feel weird at first, it will become second nature to you once you practice it for a while. Your self-talk is just as important of a daily habit as any other.

Unrealistic Expectations

Sometimes we simply just have too high of expectations that create a high world that we struggle to reach. Expecting those to be perfect and remember all the details about you is just ridiculous. If your expectations fly way above you, you are more than likely missing out on grand opportunities and are unable to truly recognize the good things that are happening that you should be celebrating.

This goes for the expectations you have for yourself as well. Are they actually realistic? If not, how can you go about making them more reasonable and achievable?

The "Should" Thoughts

Do you find your brain thinking that you "should do this" and you "should do that" often? Have you ever just taken a moment to actually find the reasoning behind why you "should"? Telling yourself that you should is equivalent to telling yourself that you are not good enough. It leads to negative self-talk fast and should be avoided. Make a positive list of the things you should do or become. Are they yours or someone else's expectations?

Taking Things Too Personally

Those with anxiety feel like many things that occur are actually their fault when in reality they more than likely had nothing to do with someone's disgruntled behavior or a glare they received. Learn to not take things too personally because you never know what may be happening in the life of other people.

"We are all in the same game, just different levels. Dealing with the same hell, just at different devils." If you think you are the cause of someone's actions, speak up and ask instead of just assuming. This will get rid of a lot of assumptions that go into negatively feeding your anxiety.

Our minds are wired to believe the things that we tell it the most. If we are always engaging in negative self-talk, expect too much of others or ourselves, do things we just merely think we "should" do or worry about those around you, your brain will act negatively as well. It is all about building a positive foundation for your frame of mind for all those thoughts of yours to dwell in. In order to unlock the door to happiness and less stress and/or anxiety, it is time to get thinking in a happy manner!

Pinpointing Your Anxiety

While you can take all the time in the world to read information in regards to relieving anxiety via the internet, books or other media, unless you take action and decide that you truly want to make a change to lower your anxiousness, it will never happen. I am an anxiety sufferer and back just a couple years ago it engulfed my everyday life and drowned me more than a few times.

I finally over time came up with a process that assisted me greatly with determining what triggered my anxious thoughts so that I could get a grip on my life and yield them from continuously taking over my personal life.

- **_Stop_** – When those feeling of anxiousness begin to hit you, stop and take a moment to make a mental note of what you are doing right at that moment. This is easier said than done, for you might be in the middle of a task, conversation, etc. But it is beneficial to take just a moment to identify when you began to feel anxious.

- **_Identify_** – Recognizing the onset of anxiety will help you come to the conclusion of what actually causes it for you personally. If you develop the capability to notice triggers and feelings when they start to dwell, you can put a stop to them faster. Many people don't realize they are feeling anxious until their symptoms are outrageously taking over them. Over time, you will be able to catch on more quickly what is threatening your happiness and overall well-being.

- **Write** – As you become an expert of taking moments to make mental notes of why you feel anxious, I find that at the end of the day I write down the events during my day, both the goods one and those that triggered my anxiety. I keep a notepad on my cellular device so that I am quickly able to access it to jot down notes at the moment and then write them down on paper before heading to bed. Be sure to write down as many details as possible – what you are thinking, experiencing and feeling, etc.

- **Analyze** – At the end of the week is when I choose to review what I have written in my anxiety notebook. You can review it at the end of each day, week or month, but I do not recommend waiting any longer than that. I wait at least a couple days to a week so that I can see the pattern that my thoughts made. When you are aware of these patterns you are better able to focus on the causes of anxiety and avoid them.

- **Possibilities** – There are numerous things that you can make the scapegoat when it comes to feeling anxious. If you have adequate knowledge of these ideas, you can review patterns and conquer anxiety. Anxiety in many cases is situational. If you are anxious being in unfamiliar surroundings, expose yourself to these types of circumstances a little time. If your causes are more based on the way you think and view the world, learn to engage in positive self-talk. Once you have a pattern written out, you will be less anxious just by the fact that you have some idea and control over your anxiety situation overall.

Chapter 3: Trauma and Anxiety

The journey of life is exciting, scary, ridiculous, confusing and worth it all at once. But there are times that we all go through some type of emotional distress, whether it be mere sadness, rapid anxiety, addictions to outside influences, obsessions with things or people, compulsions we have a hard time controlling, behaviors that are self-sabotaging, physical injuries, anger, and bleak moods, among the hundreds of other things we go through, think and/or feel.

It is important to learn ways to cope when it comes to hard times, no matter the time frame. Something psychologically downgrading can happen in a matter of mere moments and leave you scarred for the rest of your life. Some people seek out help from other individuals who are professionals at understanding the human mind, but others wish to find help within them. Having the knowledge to help yourself is not an easy feat. It may be easy to read pages upon pages of books and self-help websites that provide information, but it is much harder to put those words into actions.

The world is a much different place now than it was just a decade or two ago. Technology has advanced so rapidly that some of us are overwhelmed with it all, especially the consequences that we receive, whether from our own actions or that of another being who acted upon a current mood. Human beings are not the robots that we seem to want to create so badly these days. We are emotionally driven individuals with a lack of having the knack to help ourselves in times of need and/or trouble.

The worst thing about the constant rise of this distress is the fact that there is no one age group or certain targeted individuals that are more likely to go through it. It is happening clear from late grade school levels all the ways into senior living years. Students have much more stress with perpetual levels of testing and pressure to be better. Employees live their hard-earned careers always fighting to make their way up the ladder with not much reward. Older individuals are continuously having their wages and retirement that they worked their entire lives for whisked away.

It is a dog eat dog world out there with a lot of room to make mistakes that can cause even more friction in our personal lives. With the constant pressure to be better than the next, our society has taught us maybe how to be more proficient in terms of getting things done at school or work, but many of us have forgotten the person that is truly important: OURSELVES. If we do not take care of our emotional health, detrimental things can occur. Below are some signs that you may be experiencing emotional distress. Some of the symptoms may surprise you.

Childhood Trauma and Sensitivity to Anxiety

Trauma during childhood can impact our entire lives. According to the Journal of Affective Disorders, children who experience traumatic situations are much more likely to have anxiety and depressions and fall victim to alcohol and drug abuse. The same study found that females are more susceptible than males to develop anxiety, even with the same rates of trauma.

If left untreated, trauma during childhood can have effects that last throughout someone's entire life. They are likely to developmental disorders that branch out to much more than just anxiety as well.

Common Anxiety Disorders Caused by Trauma

Common anxiety disorders that are caused by traumatic events are:

- Panic disorder
- Obsessive Compulsive Disorder (OCD)
- Post-Traumatic Stress Disorder (PTSD)
- Body Dysmorphic Disorder

- Agoraphobia
- Social Phobia(s)

As you can imagine, trauma anytime throughout your life can play a major part in the development of anxiety and other mental disorders in your lifetime.

Chapter 4: Grabbing your life back from anxiety

Now that you have acknowledged that life could be better and have learned how to interpret why you live a life filled with anxiety, it is time to take your life back, pronto! There is a variety of methods we will discuss in this chapter that can help you gain back the confidence you need to live life to the fullest.

Managing Your Emotions

Emotions are a natural human phenomenon. , and are very present in pressing and painful times. Every day we are driven by some force of emotions:

- We take chances because we get excited about new opportunities
- We cry because we are hurting and make sacrifices for those we love

Those are just a couple examples of emotions; they dictate our actions, intentions, and thoughts with authority to our rational minds. Emotions can become a real problem, however, when we act too fast or we act on wrong types of emotions, which cause us to make rash decisions.

Negative emotions, such as bitterness, envy, or rage, are the ones that tend to spiral out of control the most, especially when triggered. It only takes one slip of our emotions to totally screw up the relationships in our lives.

If you have issues controlling your emotions, here are some steps that you can implement into your everyday life that will help you regain rationality, no matter what challenging situation you are facing:

Don't react right away

You are more likely to make mistakes when you react right away to emotional triggers. When reacting right away to these triggers, you are likely to say and do things that you will later regret.

Before acting on emotions, take a deep breath to stabilize your impulses.

Breathe deeply for just a couple minutes and you will be able to feel your heart rate return to normal. One you become calmer, remind yourself that feeling this way is just temporary.

Find healthy outlets

Once you have managed your emotions, you need to learn how to release that build up in the healthiest way possible; emotions are something that you should never let bottle up. Talk to someone you trust. Hearing their opinion of the matter can help to broaden your thoughts and regain control.

Many people keep a journal to write down how they feel. Others engage in exercise to discharge their emotions. Others meditate in order to return to their tranquil state. Whatever activity suits you, find it and use it when emotions get high.

Look at the bigger picture

All happenings in our, both bad and good, serves a purpose in our lives. Being able to see past the moment strengthens your wisdom. You may not understand certain circumstances right away, but over time, you will see the bigger picture as the pieces of the puzzle fall into order. Even when in an emotionally upsetting time, trust that there is a reason that you will comprehend in time.

Replace your thoughts

Negatively fueled emotions create negative recurring thoughts that create cycles of negative patterns over time. When confronted with these emotions, force them out of your mind and replace them with more positive thoughts. Visualize the ideal ending playing out or think about someone or something that makes you happy.

Forgive your triggers

Triggers could be the ones you love the most; you're best friend(s), your family, yourself, etc. There will be times that you may feel a sudden wave of rage when people do things that annoy you or a self-loathing feeling when you remember back to the past when you could have done thing differently. The key to managing your emotions is to first, forgive. This allows you to detach from your jealousy, fury, and resentment. As you forgive, you will discover that disassociating yourself from these feelings will do you the best.

Every day we are constantly reminded of how strong and prominent our emotions are and the power they have. We are bound to take the wrong action from time to time and feel the wrong things. To avoid acting out, simply take a few steps back and calm your spirit that is heightened from outside forces. You will be grateful for mastering your emotions when it comes to building and strengthening meaningful relationships.

Using the Power of Mini Habits

Just after Christmas in the days ending 2016, I was reflecting on the year. I realized that I had tons of room to improve but always failed at keeping up with my New Year's resolutions. Instead, I decided that in 2017, I would explore other options.

On the 28th of December, I made the choice that I wanted to get back in shape. Previously, I hardly if ever exercised and had a consistent guilt about it. My goal was a 30-minute workout, realistic, right?

I found myself unmotivated, tired, and the guilt made me feel worthless. It wasn't until a few days later that I came across a small blog article about thinking the opposite of the ideas you are stuck on. The clear opposite of my 30-minute workout goal was chilling on the couch, stuffing my face with junk food, but my brain went to the idea of 'size.'

What if, instead of carrying that guilty feeling around all the time, I just performed one push-up? I know, right? How absurd of me to think that a single push-up would do anything to help me towards my goal.

What I found was a magical secret to unlocking my potential...when I found myself struggling with my bigger goals; I gave in and did a push-up. Since I was already down on the floor, I did a few more. Once I performed a few, my muscles felt warmed up and I decided to attempt a pull-up. As you can imagine, I did several more. And soon, I exercised for entire 30-minutes!

What Are Mini Habits?

Mini habits are just like they sound; you choose a habit you want to change and you shrink them down to stupidly small tasks.

For instance, if you want to start writing at least 1,000 words per day:

- Write 50 words per day

- Read two pages of a book per day

Easy, right? I could accomplish this in 10 to 20 minutes or so. You will find that once you start meeting this daily requirement, you will far exceed them faster than you would imagine.

What is *More* Essential than Your *Habits*?

You might be wondering how you can become more comfortable in your skin and be yourself in a cruel world with these so-called mini habits. Well, think about it; what is more important than the things you do each and every day? NOTHING. Habits are responsible for 45% of how we behave, making up the foundation of who we are and how happy we are in life.

The main reason people fail to change anything in their life, even the aspects they know need to change is because they never instill new habits. Why? Simply because in the past, they have tried to do way too much, all at once. If establishing a new habit requires you to have more willpower than you can muster, you are bound to be unsuccessful. If a habit requires less willpower, you are much more likely to succeed!

Benefits of Mini Habits

There are many additional benefits that come with utilizing mini habits in your everyday life. Here are a few:

- Consistent success breeds more success
- No more guilt
- Stronger productivity
- Formation of more positively impactful habits
- Generation of motivation

Chapter 5: Belittle anxiety with personal empowerment

Having a negative attitude towards life keeps us from being happy and impacts those that we interact daily with. Science has more than enough proof to show how being positive impacts your levels of happiness and terms of success. This is why making positivity a habit with the help of small changes can help you to drastically change your overall life and the mindset you have towards the world. The life you are living is a direct reflection of your overall attitude. It can be quite easy, almost too easy, to be cynical at the world and see it as a mess of injustice and tragedy, especially thanks to the media that we all spend many hours a day on.

Negativity is holding you back from really enjoying your life and has a great impact on your environment as well. The energy that people bring to the table, including you, is very contagious. One of the best things you can do in your life that is free of charge and simplistic is to offer your positive attitude. This is especially beneficial in a world that loves and craves negativity.

One of my favorite quotes of all time comes directly from the King of Pop, Michael Jackson: *"If you want to make the world a better place, take a look at yourself and make a change."*

As humans, we are creatures of habit. In this chapter, we will outline small but significant changes that can be made to form positive habits that can drastically change the overall mindset of your life around.

Smile

When asked who we think about most of the time, the most honest answer would probably have to be ourselves, right? This is natural, so don't feel guilty! It is good to hold ourselves accountable and take responsibility for ourselves.

But I want to challenge you to put yourself aside for at least one moment per day (I recommend striving for more) and make another person smile.

Think about making someone else happy and that warm feeling you get when you receive happiness. We don't realize how intense the impact of making someone smile can have on those around us. Plus, smiling costs nothing and positively works your facial muscles!

Focus on solutions, not problems

Embracing positivity doesn't mean you need to avoid issues, but rather it is learning how to reconstruct the way you criticize. Those that are positive create criticisms with the idea to improve something. If you are just going to point out the issues with people and in situations, then you should learn to place that effort instead into suggesting possible solutions. You will find that pointing out solutions makes everyone feel more positive than pointing out flaws.

Notice the rise, not just the downfall

Many of us are negative just by the simple fact that we dwell too much on the hate and violence that is in our daily media. But what we fail to notice is those that are rising up, showing compassion, and giving love to others. Those are the stories you should engulf yourself in. When you able to find modern-day heroes in everyday life, you naturally feel more hopeful, even in tough times.

Just breathe

Our emotions are connected to the way we breathe. Think about a time that you held your breath when you were in deep concentration or when you are upset or anxious. Our breath is dependent on how we feel, which means it also has the power to change our emotions too!

Fend off other's negativity

I'm sure you have gone to work cheerful and excited to take on the day ahead, but then your co-worker ruins that happy-go-lucky mood of yours with their complaints about every little thing, from the weather to other employees, to their weekend, etc.

It is natural to find yourself agreeing to what others are saying, especially if you like to avoid conflict. But you are initially allowing yourself to drown in their pool of negative emotions. Don't fall into this trap.

Conflict may arise, but I challenge you to not validate the complaints of a friend, family member, or co-worker next time they are going about on a complaint-spree. They are less likely to be negative in the future if they have fewer people to complain to.

Switch the "*I have to*" mindset with "*I get to*"

I am sure you often fail to notice how many times we tell ourselves that we have to go and do something.

- "I have to go to work."
- "I have to go to the store."
- "I have to pay rent."
- "I have to mow the lawn."

You get the picture. But watch what happens when you swap the word have with the word get.

- "I get to go to work."
- "I get to go to the store."
- "I get to pay rent."
- "I get to mow the lawn."

See the change in attitude there? It goes from needing to fulfill those obligations to be grateful that you have those things to do in your life. This means:

- You have a job to go to
- You have enough money to support yourself and your family to provide a healthy meal
- You have a roof over your head
- You have a nice yard

When you make this simple change, you will begin to feel the warmth of happiness snuggle you like the cold blanket of stress falls away.

Describe your life positively

The choice of vocabulary we use has much more power over our lives than we realize. How you discuss your life is essential to harnessing positivity since your mind hears what you spew out loud.

When you describe your life as boring, busy, chaotic, and/or mundane, this is exactly how you will continue to perceive it and it will directly affect both your mental and physical health.

Instead, if you describe your life as involved, lively, familiar, simple, etc., you will begin to see changes in your overall perspective and you will find more joy in the way you choose to mold your entire life.

Master rejection

You will need to learn to become good at being rejected. The fact of the matter is, rejection is a skill. Instead of viewing failed interviews and broken hearts as failures, see them as opportunities for practice to ensure you are ready for what is to come next. Even if you try to avoid it, rejection is inevitable. Don't allow it to harden you from the inside out.

Rethink challenges

Stop picturing your life being scattered with dead-end signs and view all your failings as opportunities to re-direct. There are little to no things in life that we have 100-percent control over. When you let uncontrollable experiences take over your life, you will literally turn into mush.

What you can control is the amount of effort you put into things without an ounce of regret doing them! When you are able to have fun taking on challenges, you are embracing adventure and the unknown, which allows you much more room to grow, learn and win in the future.

Write in a gratitude journal

There are bound to be days where just one situation can derail the entire day, whether it be an interaction that is not so pleasant or something that happens the night before the day ahead, our mind clings to these negative aspects of the day.

I am sure you have read on multiple sites about how keeping a gratitude journal is beneficial. If you are anything like me, I thought this was total rubbish that is until I started doing it. I challenged myself to write down at least five things that I was truly grateful for each and every day. Scientifically, expressing gratitude is linked to happiness and reducing stress.

I challenge you to begin jotting down things you appreciate and are grateful for each day. Even on terrible days, there is something to be blessed about!

Chapter 6: Everyday techniques to fend off anxiety

Despite the toll that anxiety and its symptoms can have on everyday life and fulfillment, in today's world there are many different techniques and methods you can learn to incorporate into your everyday routine that help you to control and possibly even eliminate anxiety from your life. Each section of this chapter will be dedicated to a specific genre of techniques that anyone has the ability to learn!

Visualization and Anxiety

Seeing *is* believing, which is a key secret to how entrepreneurs and well-known people in society stand out and achieve success and fulfill their dreams. *Visualization is the simple use of imagination through mental imagery to help form visions of what we want in our lives and how we can make them a reality.*

There are two main kinds of visualization:

Pragmatic Visualization represents a set of days that helps to gain new ideas and interpret what it says/means to them. It helps those understand structures that lie within a set of data.

Artistic Visualization is similar to pragmatic in that it utilizes visuals to convey information but in a different sense. It is used to show people that data is being monitored carefully and shows particular aspects of data that is connected to one another to depict an entire idea.

So, how does learning about these two kinds of visualization help you in your quest to decrease anxiety? Well, visual techniques help to drastically overcome symptoms of anxiety. When the two types are combined, visualization is powerful in obtaining and staying in a calmer state of mind.

When it comes to anxiety, visualization requires one to picture themselves in a safe, peaceful and/or tranquil environment. Anywhere that makes you happier is where you should be imagining yourself during visualization exercises. It does sound pretty funny at first glance, but trust me when I say there is something about being able to transport your mind to somewhere mentally tranquil. Not only will your mind thank you but your body will too, for it becomes much more relaxed and stress-free when performing these practices. Visualization gives people something to distract themselves from the current world that surrounds them.

Why You Should Be Using Visualization

Beyond visualization itself, you can literally view the best of life from the comfort of your own couch. This chapter will showcase the benefits that come with the dedicated practice of learning and incorporating ways of visualization into your everyday life.

- **Improved quality of relationships** – The positive outcomes of utilizing visualization doesn't just end within yourself. Since you are developing a better mindset that aids in your views and beliefs, those around you will like and appreciate the more confident, positive you!

- **Boosts your mood** – When one practices the methods of visualization, they naturally experience a sort of joy that is quite unexplainable to some. Once you finish one of these sessions successfully, you will more than likely feel boastfully happy, calm and relaxed.

- **Relieves stress** – Practicing the ways of visualization naturally causes one to be able to relax. It has a way of quieting the mind to be able to think happier, more positive thoughts which tone down loads of stress that pile on our shoulders almost on a daily basis.

- **Strengthens the immune system** – Thanks to all that dialing down of stress and things that fuel stress, your body is better able to fight off sickness which makes you physically better, longer. This also helps in aiding anxiety because you are not constantly worrying about getting ill all the time as well.

- **Ability to learn new things quicker** – When the mind is in a calmer state, it is able to pick up and grasp new concepts much easier than when it is bogged down with so many negative thoughts and emotions.

- **Able to cope with the feeling of nervousness** – When you take time out of your day to practice visualization, you are initially settling all those negative feelings that you may have about yourself and what others may think of you as well. This immensely helps individuals who are naturally more nervous combat that feeling, which leaves room to try and experiment with new things and ideas. Imagine yourself in a great looking outfit giving that inevitable speech that is due soon. Then imagine an applauding audience. It is quite the confidence booster!

- **Builds stronger concentration skills** – Visualization makes room for your mind to do other tasks efficiently by spring cleaning negative thoughts, feelings, emotions, and past experiences. This doesn't mean it is responsible for getting rid of them 100%, but it helps one to be able to cope and bring down those bad levels to make room for productivity.

- **Assists in overcoming recurring issues** – When the weight of your entire world is upon your shoulders, it is no wonder that we begin to believe that our lives were just made to be a laughing-stalk to some because of how life's unlucky events have left us feeling. This can lead to long-term problems and beliefs. Visualization combats these two things.

- **Can give you a spark of inspiration** – During your sessions, if your mind always veers to one idea in particular, perhaps it is time to take initiative and proceed with the steps in achieving it! Visualizing doing something can directly inspire you to do as such.

- **Makes one more creative** – Visualization not only takes concentration but also a truckload of creativity as well. If you are going to picture something in detail and add the other four senses to that visual, you have to really want to mold it into reality. We all have creative bones in our bodies. Visualization just brings them out more, honing that skill and letting it shine.

- **No boundaries** – As I have mentioned before, when it comes to visualization, practice makes perfect. Just like with any newly acquired skill, one must learn to hone its practice to be able to tweak it when needed and use it to their utmost advantage. With certain visualization techniques, you can literally picture yourself doing something that would otherwise be usually hard to achieve. With those images in mind, you then have a good idea what you must do to actually and realistically accomplish that image you had in your head during a visualization session. This method knows no bounds!

- **Method of practice and rehearsal** – Believe it or not, visualization can be a way to practice your favorite sport or nail that upcoming work pitch that you have been reciting and memorizing for days. Picturing yourself doing or performing something is just as effective as actually completing the task at hand. Utilizing visualization with real, physical practice can get you to honing that skill or memorizing things much quicker.

- **Picture yourself getting stronger and healthier** – Sounds unbelievable, but if you are sick, seeing yourself get better will have the result of getting healthier, sooner. Visualization reduces stress and relaxes your mind, which also assists in healing your body of sickness or physical injury as well. This allows your body to function at its full capacity. You would be surprised what our bodies could accomplish in a day's work if we treated them more like the temples they are and should always be. It is safe to say we take our physical presence for granted most days. And it tends to show more often than not!

- **Gives us joy** – Many people who practice the ways of visualization tend to picture something that brings them happiness. We almost are never quite in the right place or time in our lives to always have what we want and that is okay! But that doesn't mean we shouldn't get the luxury of seeing it for ourselves, right? Picturing a goal or what we want the most from life can bring us quite a load of temporary happiness if one wants to view it that way. Why temporary? If you can picture it, you can eventually and more than likely make it happen in your future, which is why visualization can be a great motivator.

Aspects of Successful Visualization Practices

There are three aspects to successfully become one with visualization:

- **Practice** – Learning the ways of visualization may actually be more stressful and frustrating for beginners because it is not a practice we are naturally keen to perform. Those that start practicing visualization have a false sense of what the experience is supposed to feel like and have false expectations about the outcome. This inhibits the practice from really taking effect. Visualization is something that has to be practiced daily to work for you long-term. If practiced the right way, it will eventually become second nature to you but only if you really dedicate yourself to learning its ways and practicing it every day until you have it down pat.

- **Utilizes ALL the senses** – Visualization doesn't just use your sense of how a certain peaceful place appears to you in your mind. You have to imagine what your safe space smells, tastes sounds and feels like as well. The more detailed you are in regards to your senses, the better visualization you will have and the more relaxed you can potentially become.

- **Actions** – All human beings experience mental barriers that keep them from being happy and the process of practicing and performing visualization is not excluded from this. Even for visualizing experts, bad thoughts from the course of one's day can inhibit one from getting a clear vision of their safe haven. You have to find a way to release and/or transform those bad thoughts and feelings into something that you can tangibly get rid of.

Forms of Visualization for Anxiety

Visualization is a skill that can be utilized to obtain a better life, especially for those that suffer from an anxiety disorder. Now, we will talk about techniques in the visualization world. Although all of these are not for everyone, try them out and see what works for you.

Meditation

Meditation is a superb form of apathetic visualization that can lead to very powerful results. Visualizing through means of meditation is more of an outgrowth than the main focus. When you begin to incorporate meditation sessions into your everyday routine, you will gradually be opening the door to your inner self, which will then lead you to be able to visualize more clearly and easily.

The more experience you have with meditation, the smoother sessions become and the more you get to see and take away from your visions. It is important not to become frustrated with yourself or discouraged from continuing to practice meditation if you are just starting out.

The whole point of meditation is to empty your brain of thoughts and feelings and to let your mind wander to wherever it wants to go. A vital component of meditation is breathing. Learn to focus on how you take in and let out breaths of air. Let your mind veer off to wherever its little heart desires. Once you begin to practice this technique more often, it will become easier and faster to exhaust your mind of concerns or other worries and let other things come in and explore. It will become second nature for you to sit down, relax and get into a clear state of mind so that you can visualize to your contentment.

Meditation makes way for things that you never thought were actually within you. Once you rid your brainwaves of all that noise from the course of your day, thoughts occur at their own pace.

Altered Memory Visualization

This visualization technique targets past memories and learning how to change them to a more positive standpoint. For those with anxiety about things that stem from their past, this is especially helpful in obtaining a brighter state of mind. This technique is one to utilize if you are one that holds on to past anger and resentment from particular situations that you finally want to rid yourself of.

No one can change the past, but you can teach your brain how it views these past scenarios in your mind. Get into a calmed state and visualize the scenario that you wish had a different outcome. Restore things said that were fueled by anger with comments that are controlled and peaceful. This does take some time and you may have to revisit this scene in your head multiple times to nail the outcome that you wish had resulted from the past situation. It is recommended to not do this day upon day in a row, but rather space out revisiting the scene.

Over time, your brain will begin to only recall what YOU have recreated, making a once painful or uncomfortable situation fade away in memory. Try to imagine little cubicle offices in each major section of your brain. In this instance, I like to picture a little office guy that is in charge of just the bad memories. During these sessions, you are instructing him on how to rewrite particular events that have occurred in the past and once they are rewritten the way you once anticipated them to play out, this office dude can start to shred your memories of these occurrences.

Receptive Visualization

This technique is much like viewing a movie inside your head, but you are the director of the scenes within this movie. Get yourself to a quiet space, lie back, get comfortable and close your eyes. Focus on building the scene in which you want to see acted out in your mind.

Once a clear backdrop and scenery is within your mind, place people, noises, smells and sounds within your scene of this movie. It is best to slowly build your way up to the actual scene until you are comfortable and content with it, then it is time for action! Focus on feeling involved within this scene of your "movie."

Treasure Map

This visualization technique not only uses mental fundamentals but also physical components as well. You will need to have an idea of what you want to visualize before getting to the nitty-gritty of performing this method. Start by using your art skills to draw out some type of physical representation of the components you need to achieve in order to reach your ultimate goal.

For example, perhaps you have an upcoming test that you want to get a great grade on. Draw out a building symbolizes a school, a book that you will need to use to study for this test and then a representation of yourself. Try to make your drawing detailed, but do not worry about the maturity of your art abilities too much here. It is not the drawings themselves that are important, but rather what you are imagining WHILE sketching them out.

As you draw out your "map to success", your mind is actually visualizing ways that will get you to where you want to be. Patience is a key with this particular technique, for it does take a bit of time to truly become completely mentally occupied in this exercise. It is crucial to take your notepad and pen to a quiet space and to not be around anything distracting such as a radio, television, people or phones.

How to Design Your Own "Safe Space"

Safe places or spaces are a mind's sanctuary, created for the purpose of retreat if one needs a mental location to be able to visualize or hone their meditative state and reduce stress. Creating one of these is kind of like personalizing a physical space in your home. You want to do anything to truly make it YOURS.

It can be anything from a room inside an imaginary home, a room in your realistic home that you want to visualize differently, the beach, a comforting outdoorsy area, etc. As you meditate or relax and begin to dive deeper into your imagery or visualization session, this is the place you imagine you want to go. It is anywhere that you wish to return to time after time, so put some effort and thought into where you will always find comfort in mentally retreating to.

- **Brainstorm** – The goal is to develop a place that you feel calm, content and happy within, no matter the reason that you retreat to it. If you have difficulty seeking out such a place, start by looking through art, magazines, books, old photographs, etc. Always lean towards ideas that burst with positivity for you.

- Are you more apt to feel calmer in an outdoor/natural setting or do you feel better within the walls of some type of structure?

- Are there pieces of writing such as within books, poems of stories that make you feel at ease?

- Do you feel more comforted by populated areas or tranquil areas?

- **Think of a time where you felt happy and safe** – Memories are the best areas to seek things that bring joy to you. Think back to memories that you were happy, content, playful, peaceful, etc. Write these down in detail. It could be literally anywhere, as long as it brought contentment to you.

  - Where did this memory occur?
  - How old were you?
  - Why did this memory make you happy?
  - Who was with you within this memory?

- **Create various rooms** – Your safe space does not necessarily have to be just 2D, one room vision. It can have various sections, compartments or rooms within it. This allows you to trek to different areas throughout your visualization sessions. This also allows one the ability to be able to compartmentalize issues and deal with them one part at a time.

  - *Fill your space with cherished people* – There are many individuals that would rather be alone while in their safe place, while others prefer the company of their favorite people. Imagine who makes you happy and during the course of a visualization session, imagine greeting them and welcoming them into your safe space. This also goes for people in your life that may have passed away that you miss and wish to see. Having conversations with them and asking for advice could make a world of difference!

- *Utilize ALL your senses* – Seeing is believing, but visions of your safe place are a lot more believable and turn in better results if you learn to engage all your senses while within them. Engulf yourself in tastes, sounds smells and how things feel between your fingers and toes and against your skin. It will enhance your visualization experience ten-fold.

- *Write out all the details* – Once you have taken the dedicated time to develop and build your safe place, write down all the tiniest details that you can remember. Writing in a lot of detail can assist you in returning to that place in your mind easier and more efficiently. Some individuals even videotape, sculpt, draw or paint out their descriptions for safekeeping for future use.

  - Are there animals or people?
  - What do you feel?
  - How small or big is your space?
  - What colors?
  - What surrounds you?
  - What is the ultimate backdrop or setting?

- **Visualize positive results** – The main rule of thumb for visualization is imagining situations acted out in positive manners. This involves a heavy amount of thinking happily and setting up a content scene. Imaging positive outcomes are really just a more in-depth version of regular run-of-the-mill positive thinking.

Developing Anxiety Routines

Anxiety routines are any type of daily routine that you use to calm yourself down in stressful situations and that leaves you feeling physical, mental or emotionally distressed. These routines are meant to help you bounce back from the depths of your own thoughts and live a life full of more passion and fulfillment.

This means it is very crucial to choose routines that not only suit you but are healthy, too. Life runs smoother when you have a routine to fulfill those nasty little voices in your head or when you feel like you may make a bad choice because of your anxiety symptoms. Sadly, some people choose unhealthy habitual routines that not only push them back into a negative state but may even provoke symptoms of anxiety and make them worse.

These bad routines could be anything from drug use, both illegal and prescription, large consumption of alcohol or heavy smoking of cigarettes, etc. You get the picture. Creating an anxiety routine for yourself should not include things that will cause you greater harm in the long run. Honestly, habits like those stated above are only going to make your symptoms worse.

As human beings, we are automatically wired to detect any sort of negative energy that may cause us harm. Anxiety becomes so bad within certain people simply because our bodies do not quite know the difference between stressful triggers that are actually harmless to us versus actual, life-threatening aspects that may be sprung upon us.

Our bodies are made to react to protect ourselves. This is why being mentally prepared for the day that lies ahead of you is so crucial, especially for anxiety sufferers. It is important to back up our thoughts with an extra layer of positivity to promote a sense of safety and well-being. This is much easier said than done, especially when life may not have been a very good friend to you as of late. But being able to mentally develop a positive sense of self is the first step in creating daily routines that help pave your way to a successful life to live and your future.

Routines to Decrease Anxiety

With the right amount of inspiration, the first day or two of adding a new routine to your life can be exciting. You know you are making a positive change that will hopefully help you feel better about yourself and the life you live. However, self-care routines can be a hard thing to manage and utilize on a regular basis once the newness of acting upon it wears off.

Anxiety can leave some sufferers so dismayed by anxious or sad thoughts that they want nothing more than to do away with anything that resonates positive energy. But this is the exact opposite of fighting for yourself and your happiness. Everyone has their bad days and moments and by all means, you are allowed to have and live those. But it is important not to stay tucked away in them for long periods of time.

Developing and executing specific daily routines that you are comfortable with gives those a step by step plan for the day and keeps you prepared for situations or other anxiety triggers from leaping out and mugging you of your happiness. Routines, kind of like exercise, are things we practice daily to keep us in shape, but anxious routines keep our minds in check. You never know when something will catch you off guard, when a person may ask you something that is bothersome or when a debilitating symptom of anxiety will hit you throughout the course of the day. It is better to be prepared than not to be, right?

The Importance of a Balanced Morning Routine

Many functions within routines do them absolutely no good. When the alarm goes off, they tend to hit snooze a few times. When they finally decide to open their eyes, they automatically reach for their phones and look at updates on social media. Many people are already let down by the fact no one messaged them or liked their posts throughout the night.

When their feet finally touch the floor to stand up out of bed, they are already on a path to a negative, self-destructing day. They take a quick shower, down a bowl of cereal and chug a cup of coffee and get to their day job...what is the point?

This lack of routine is non-beneficial. We see our unstructured lives as having no real purpose, which results in a lack of inner peace. We are destroying our happiness without realizing it!

Benefits of a Morning Routine

Creating a morning routine is not only a big part in relieving anxiety, but it also boosts productivity, brings out your inner positivity, helps you to develop and successfully sustain good relationships, as well as being a big reducer of negativities. Morning routines alone have been shown to be the best strategy for reducing stress and relieving those pesky symptoms of anxiety, no matter how long they have resided within you.

Morning routines keep you consciously aware and more grounded throughout the day. In fact, many who were once stubborn and did not want to incorporate a daily routine were eventually surprised at how much better they felt each and every morning. Anxiety levels dropped and confidence and happiness levels substantially rose. A morning routine can literally reduce your anxiety by as much as sixty percent!

Steps to Include in Your Morning Routine

When you **wake up earlier,** you know that you have plenty of time to get up and get ready for your day, which aids in decreased stress levels. If there is adrenaline pumping throughout your body as you rush around to head out the door, it sticks with you for the rest of the day.

Sounds like a waste of time, but **making your bed each morning** is a powerful task that helps you gain the momentum you need to get pumped for the day ahead. For those that suffer from anxiety and depression, making the bed is simple but can make a huge difference because you know you have completed *one* task if not anything else.

Meditation and prayer is a subject with many critics. People view meditation as an act performed only by spiritual individuals. Practicing mindfulness daily has positive side effects that can trigger feel-good hormones in the brains that aid in reducing levels of stress, anxiety and even depression.

Mixing meditation and prayer within your morning routine can be quite vitalizing, giving clarity to your life and your decisions. If you wish to learn more about the power behind the act of prayer, it will be covered in the following chapter The Empowerment of Prayer.

Taking an ice cold shower in the mornings has been proven to provide the human body with a great number of benefits. Cold exposure, also known as cold shower therapy, is nothing new. Our ancestors utilized it as a remedy to treat mental ailments. Showering in cold water provides the body with adequate circulation and tones the skin nicely.

The cold feeling kicks positive responses throughout the body into overdrive. It accelerates the repairing of cells, which reduces inflammation, pain, and speeds up our metabolic processes. The icy waters help lower negative levels that depression and anxiety can hover over us. Standing under the cold water for just a couple minutes can yield you these benefits.

Substitute your breakfast with coffee or tea to bump up energy levels and replace your usual breakfast eats. This is not recommended for absolutely everyone, but if you are trying to find ways to keep hunger away for the first portion of your day, give it a shot!

Learn how to **utilize a journal** to make "morning pages" as part of your routine in the mornings. This is my personal favorite way to "mind dump" any curious or troubling thoughts you had during the previous day and the night before, as well as random ideas that pop into your mind. I write in my journal after taking a shower, since great ideas tend to spring during those few minutes. When you are able to write down all the negative feelings on paper, you can then get through the day with a clearer state of mind.

Practice gratitude by jotting down things you would miss if they were no longer in your life, such as objects, people, etc. into your morning pages.

To start the day on a positive note, **jot down what you are looking forward** to that day. This tells our brains to look up, think up and be bright and helps to relieve anxiety.

Write down your intentions at the beginning of each day, no matter how corny they may sound, such as *"I will choose to be consciously present today."*

Write out important tasks that you wish to achieve during the day to ensure you will feel prepared and have a fulfilling plan. This will ease your mind so that you can develop a clear path of action to achieving that days' goals.

I know I have mentioned writing a lot, but like I said before it is a powerful tool. Every morning our brains are ready to go and on high alert, so it is good to have a well-thought-out plan of action.

Write down at least three to five of the most important tasks that you have to complete. Focus on ones that stress you out just thinking about them. Then, ask yourself the following questions about the tasks you have jotted out so that you can prioritize them accordingly:

- Which tasks will help me inch closer to achieving my main goal?

- What task do I have the most fearful anxious thoughts about?

- Which tasks have the potential to cancel out others if done successfully?

Spend 90 minutes every day working towards accomplishing your priorities. Targeting your main goals during the morning hours help you to get them accomplished productively.

Other Morning Methods to Relieve Anxiety

Play uplifting music to ensure an upbeat, positive mood. Create a playlist to play throughout your morning routine. Make your phone's alarm tone a good song to wake up to. You would be surprised at what a difference this effortless step takes.

Spend time with a pet(s) to help raise your dopamine and serotonin levels, resulting in lessened anxiety and depression. Pets also motivate us to climb out of bed and give us the initiative to take on the day, even when our anxiety tries to get the best of us. Adding them to your morning routine is a bonus for not only you but for your pet's well-being too!

Change your scenery in simple ways; Go outside, take a walk. Visit your favorite café and grab a coffee. Go out with a friend. The longer you dwell in a space that sucks away happiness, the worse you will feel.

Interactions with the outside world can be enough to distract you from your anxious habits. This is another reason routines are so important in aiding anxiety. Avoiding responsibilities can actually damage you mentally more than you realize. It is good to get your attention off the darkness of life that resides inside your head. It only makes your anxiety worse when you sit around and obsess over it.

Coping with anxiety and its symptoms can lead to a life of great discomfort. Having some type of structure in the form of routines can be quite crucial to one's success in living a happy, go-lucky life. The next few chapters will cover other types of routines in detail that can help relieve and maybe even make your symptoms disappear for good! It is all about you to initiate making the change.

Chapter 7: Transforming Your anxiety for a better life

If you are feeling anxious or depressed about your future and are allowing negative thoughts to get the best of you and dampen your motivation for success, then learning to use anxiety to your advantage is a must.

Personally, I have learned to *choose* to view my anxiety has a valuable asset that yields me to lead a more authentic life. I live empathetically, for my anxiety has made me a vulnerable person and thus, helped me deepen my life's relationships.

Having anxiety just means I am not mellow enough to take things for granted in life, therefore, making life a richer experience all the way around. In fact, there are a few inspirational ways that anxiety has helped me to elevate my life:

- Got me actively involved in personal development
- Taught me how to think in the present and act now
- Got me reading more books and discover how it heals the mind
- Started me on tracking my success and not just on failure
- Taught me how to make a positive game out of my life
- Assisted me to take control over my life
- Reconnected me to the habit of learning new things every day
- Showed me the power of meditation and visualization
- Allowed me to see that I am not the only one in my life that suffers from degrees of anxiety
- Has taught me to be a more actively vulnerable person

Using Anxiety to Your Advantage

Believe it or not, anxiety can be used for good and can be a powerful force in motivating yourself to achieve your desires. Using stress to add momentum to your life is constructive, instead of allowing it to deconstruct our lives.

Redefining danger

You must learn to see anxiety differently; anxiety, before our brains get a
hold of it and dwell, is just a warning sign used for our survival. At this point,
you are allowing anxiety to make you feel panicked. But even when that
warning sign lights up, it doesn't mean you are in danger. You must save this
energy for when you really need to make quick decisions.

Create a list of less to most dangerous to help identify a good spectrum of
threats. With that comparison, you will be able to see what "dangerous"
situations are safe and which ones are frightening.

Channel your stress properly

Diamonds don't grow from trees; they are coals that turn into something
more beautiful through pressure. Channeling stress positively into energy for
motivation does take time and can be physically and emotionally draining.
But instead of allowing negative thoughts take hold of you and send you
down that same spiraling hole of anxiety, look at the situation before you
differently; view it as your time to *shine*! When negativity starts to manifest in
your mind, challenge those thoughts. When you challenge them, you will find
that the negativity in them is totally empty in the first place.

Stop trying to do your best

There are two kinds of people: those that do their best and those that can *do
better*. However, those that strive to do their best constantly are the ones that
end up emotionally drained than those who do better. Why? Because when
you do your best, you are settling. When you strive to *do better*, you accept that
you are not doing as good as you know you can. For anxiety sufferers, what

they do isn't good enough for them. They either drown in their shortcomings or have learned to take the opportunity to improve themselves.

In those with anxiety, underestimation is a common cognitive distortion. When we tell ourselves that we can do better, we know how to reject our deficiencies and go out of their way to prove themselves wrong.

Chapter 8: Battling anxiety like a true warrior

"The only thing we have to fear is fear itself."

- *President Theodore Roosevelt*

Marines, SEALs, and Special Forces have no choice but to face life-threatening danger head-on regularly. The fact is, if they do get caught up in fear, they are more likely to lose their lives. While many of us will thankfully never have to face these experiences, why aren't we using the fear-crushing tactics that they use in our own personal lives?

Spend time preparing

If you are worried about a work presentation, stressing over a job interview, or freaking out about the upcoming rap battle that might help you move out of your mom's house, then stop, prepare, and practice instead of sitting around. The key is to lose yourself in the moment, which you to by devoting a ton of energy into preparing for what you are worried about. Spend 75% preparing and 25% for the actual event.

SEALs are able to erase fear by practicing upcoming mission until they feel naturally confident. When the unknown becomes more known to them, they don't have to lie to themselves about the risks, but instead put themselves in a better position to handle the unknown, which develops confidence.

Learn to *manage* fear

One of the best ways to deal with fear is to laugh about it. What? You read that right! Laughter lets you know that things are going to be okay and work out. Don't worry; there is evidence to back this theory up. A study by Stanford University showed that those that were trained to make jokes to respond to negative images. This is a much healthier way to deal with fear. The world is an inevitably twisted place, so seeing the funnier side of things makes it easier to deal with.

Breathe

When your heart is beating from your chest, your joints turn into Jell-O, and sweat is pouring off your face, then the best thing you can do to calm the physical manifestations of fear derived from anxiety is to breathe.

That simple? YES. By just inhaling for four seconds and exhaling for four seconds, SEALs can calm their nervous systems and maintain control of their natural biological responses to fear.

You are essentially bending your body's software to better control the hardware. In other words, you are giving yourself a pretty bomb superpower! Breathing helps the body go from the fight-or-flight response of the sympathetic nervous system to the relaxed response of the parasympathetic nervous system.

Tactical breathing used by Navy SEALS for performance just prior to a tense situation or during a workout:

Breathe through the nose. It's very important to breathe through your nose since breathing through the nose stimulates nerve cells that exist behind sternum near the spine that triggers the parasympathetic nervous system. Anxiety is a sympathetic response and parasympathetic counteracts that. This calms your body, which then calms your mind.

1. Relaxed sitting position and right handle on the belly.
2. Activate the breath by pushing belly out and then inhale deeply for a count of four. Inhale to the belly. This pulls breath deep into the lungs. Exhale through the nose for a count of four, pulling the belly button toward the spine. Repeat this three times.
3. Now breathe in through belly and diaphragm for a count of four, again inhaling into your belly and this time lifting your chest. Again, exhale

for a count of four so that your rib cage falls and your belly button pulls toward your spine. Repeat three times.

4.   Next, use the same technique, this time inhaling for a count of four through the belly, diaphragm and your chest, with a slight raise of shoulders for inhaling. Exhale for a count of four three the chest, diaphragm, and then the belly. Repeat three times, eventually working your breaths up to eight counts.

Next, box breathing is a technique used by the U.S. Navy SEALS to maintain focus and to calm nervous system after a tense situation, such as combat, an intense workout or anytime the desire is to center and focus.

Trains for diaphragmic breathing or deep breathing. Relaxes the whole system and provides oxygen to the brain to focus better. Improves energy. It can also be used by you to regain your sense of balance, concentration, and relaxation and can be practiced at any time. Use the same technique as tactical breathing but you use a five-count hold between breaths.

1.   Get in a relaxed sitting position

2.   Inhale deeply through the nose for five seconds

3.   Hold the air in your lungs for five seconds

4.   Exhale for five seconds, releasing all the air from your lungs

5.   Hold your lungs empty for five seconds

6.   Repeat for five minutes, or as long as you feel necessary

Don't keep things bottled up

Fear is just like terrible liquor; it sucks when you drink it and has negative effects that last a long time, which is why it is important to deal with it before and after the fact.

Talking about scary experiences helps soldiers locate the meaning behind it all. This communication allows them to process what they have been through positively and helps them to create closer relationships with their mates. Scared? Admit it to a friend. Hearing it out loud can help you pull it out, confront it, and deal with it.

Overpower that inner nagging voice

We are all aware of the inner chatter that occurs in our mind on a daily basis. In fact, our inner voice can be really negative the majority of the time. Wouldn't it be cool to have an inner monologue that reminds us how confident and awesome we are? Wouldn't it be great to have an inner motivational speaker to get us through tough times?

Well, you can. In times of stress, our brains are wired to create self-talk that can increase our feelings of fear. As a soldier, they are expected to fight against their inner self-talk and focus on positive portions of experiences. With practice, they are easily able to ignore or even erase the negativity their brains are throwing at them. So, you can do the same in your own life.

Fear and anxiety thrive when we imagine the worst. We developed imagination to be able to project into the future so we can plan ahead. However, a side effect of being able to imagine possible positive futures is being able to imagine things going wrong. A bit of this is useful; after all, there really might be muggers or loan sharks. But uncontrolled imagination is a testing ground for anxiety and fear that can spoil otherwise happy lives.

Some people misuse their imagination chronically and so suffer much more anxiety than those who either future-project their imaginations constructively or who don't tend to think about the future much at all. Anxious, chronic worriers tend to misuse their imaginations to the extent that upcoming events feel like catastrophes waiting to happen. No wonder whole lives can be blighted by fear and anxiety.

Think of the worst-case scenario

No matter what you are afraid of, you always have the opportunity to avoid it for the rest of your life. However, soldiers don't get that choice. They face similar situations time and time again that scare them. To ensure fear doesn't overrule them, they simulate stressful scenarios and try to experience the emotions with them as well.

Instead of thinking happy thoughts and ignoring what you are afraid of, start looking at the worst things that can possibly happen. When you are able to picture the worst fear and stay within an emotional experience instead of pushing yourself out of it, your mind tends to get over the fear naturally.

Reframe your mindset

Reframe you definition of symptoms. Reframe the symptoms of anxiety - give them a different meaning. Those sweaty palms, racing heart, and lightheadedness can mean a panic attack or they can mean the most exciting and fun adventure of your life! Your body doesn't know the difference and it is just doing what it does by nature, but you can choose how you define that sudden rush. Don't believe me?

How do you think those adrenaline junkies dives off cliffs, jump motorcycles or swim with sharks? Their definition of what we call fear is definitely different. They still experience the same potent chemicals coursing through their body, but the sensations have a different meaning to them. What you experience as fear, dread and near death can be defined as thrilling, exciting, and aliveness to someone else.

The beautiful thing about consistently and purposely redefining these symptoms is you can actually rewire your brain. This leads us to neuroplasticity.

Neuroplasticity

Neuroplasticity occurs with changes in behavior, thinking, and emotions. With conscious practice, we can alter our neural pathways to move naturally towards our desired emotions, such as being thankful, calm, and happy and away from anger, stress, and panic.

As you choose to respond with positive emotion, you can strengthen the neural pathways to the desired emotions. As you make more neural connections over time to your desired emotion, the pathways to the negative reactions eventually become weaker and scrambled. This even works while using mental rehearsals of the situation and practicing your desired response.

Remember, this can also work in reverse. If you have a habitual response to circumstances, such as being angry in a traffic jam and you repeat these responses over and over in a high state of emotion, you will strengthen the neural pathways towards the emotion of anger in that situation. The masters over the centuries who taught positive thinking and faith may have actually been on to something and now we can prove it scientifically.

Get moving

Exercise is usually associated with weight loss, improved physical health, and a stronger immune system. But the benefits of exercise can expand much more. Exercise is just as important for your mental fitness as it is your physical health. Aerobic activity promotes the release of endorphins that are released in the brain and act as painkillers, which also help to increase a sense of well-being. Endorphins also improve energy levels, provide a better night's sleep, elevate your mood and provide anti-anxiety effects. Exercise also takes your mind off of your worries and breaks the cycle of negative thoughts that contribute to anxiety.

It is recommended to perform 30 minutes or more of exercise five days a week to have a significant impact on anxiety symptoms. You don't need a formal exercise program at the gym to experience these benefits. Light physical activity has been shown to have the same effects, including gardening, housework, washing the car and walking around the block. These can be done in small intervals throughout the day.

It's more important to do some sort of physical activity on a consistent basis than to aim for something that is not sustainable. Be realistic and if you need to start with smaller goals, do so. This is all about taking care of yourself in a way that works for you.

The single, most important natural tool you can use to beat anxiety is regular exercise. It sounds cliché, but the truth is that exercise affects the mind and body in ways that science is still discovering.

There is a reason that anxiety prevalence has grown with our increasingly inactive lifestyles. Jogging every day can make a world of difference in how you deal with stress, how your anxiety symptoms manifest, and how you regulate your mood.

The best methods of exercise to combat anxiety are:

- **Running** releases feel-good hormones that have exponential mental health benefits. It can help you fall asleep faster, improve memory, lower stress levels, and protects against developing depression.

- **Hiking** in a wooded or hilly location has natural calming effects on the brain. Being around plants and Earthly sights helps to reduce anxiety thanks to the chemicals plants emit. Plus, being out in nature is great for your health and memory function.

- **Yoga,** a lot like meditation, has been found to significantly reduce anxiety and other neurotic symptoms that can lead to irritability and depression. It not only strengthens your core but helps you to focus on breathing, which is the key to relaxing the mind and combating anxiety.

Chapter 9: Rediscovering yourself after hurricane anxiety

Those that live with and through the darkness of anxiety can find themselves waking up each day unhappy. Life is short and there comes a time where re-evaluating your life in order to revamp parts of it to ensure your happiness and fulfillment.

We all get lost in life from time to time. We forget old passions we had, give up interest in pursuit of something else, etc. But it is never too late to rediscover what makes you great and what makes you feel truly alive.

When were you the *happiest?*

Take a moment to remember when you were the most content with your life. In high school? College? Before marriage, family, and kids? When you began your family? Started your business? Pursued a new hobby?

No one peaks at the same time or levels in their lives. The key to regaining contentment is not to think of those fond times as "the past", but to figure out how to find that feeling of happiness again where you currently are in your life. How can you re-incorporate those things that brought you joy in the life you are living now?

What makes you *unhappy?*

What makes your blood pressure shoot through the roof? Figuring out the things that push your last buttons is just as important as knowing what helps you keep a positive outlook. When you are able to clearly point out the toxic influences, you will be better able to erase them and develop better, healthier ways of living. We tend to hold onto things from the past that has negative impacts on our current lives. What grudges are you holding onto? These are toxic and are keeping you from being your best self! No matter what it is, from a toxic ex-partner to a job that drains you, cutting these negative influences will allow you ample space to grow in a positive direction.

Write!

When negative thoughts are constantly bouncing around the brain, it can be very easy to become overwhelmed. We tend to forget how much our daily thoughts impact our lives. They take hold of our power, telling us who we are and what are and aren't capable of. We are the only ones that have the power to take action to erase pesky thoughts from inhibiting our success in life.

I have found that organizing thoughts by writing them down makes them more abstract. When you can visualize them on paper, it makes them concrete.

Write out a list of pros and cons, random thoughts that pop up, poetry, grocery lists, anything that comes to mind. All writing can be therapeutic and helps us to rediscover how our voice sounds, which radiates who. I challenge to find yourself again with the power of good old pen and paper.

Learning to Love Yourself Again

To rediscover yourself, you need to learn how to love yourself again for who you are, and all parts of yourself, including your flaws and everything you have endured. There are millions of places that offer up 'good advice' to practice self-love, but they never explain exactly how to do so.

Loving yourself is a vital piece of the puzzle when it comes to positive personal growth. It allows us to fulfill our dreams and create happy and healthy relationships with others too.

Care about yourself as much as you care about others

This sounds almost too simple, but many of us are not selfish enough when it comes to fulfilling our wants and needs. It is hard to remember that you are **not** selfish when it comes to caring about yourself and your wellbeing.

Showing yourself compassion shows those in your life that you are able to take care of yourself. No one can pour from an empty pot, which means you need to take care of yourself in order to take care of others in your life. Treat yourself the way you treat your best friend, with caring, concern, and gentleness, no matter what is happening in your life.

Maintain boundaries

Jot down a list of things you need emotionally, both what is important to you and what upsets you. The list can be made up of anything, from wanting sympathy to being celebrated, to being cared for, etc. Whatever is important to you, no matter how silly it sounds, **Write. It. Down.**

We can often find ourselves smack dab in the middle of the confusing conflict and wonder how we got there in the first place. We ask ourselves how we attracted this situation and the people in it with us. While you still need to take responsibility for your actions, it is also crucial to not fall into a pit of self-blame that can cause stress, but rather really look into what is occurring. Many people lack inner confidence and have no idea what they are worth. This lack can leave us living in a sum-zero equation; we are loved completely or become completely unlovable.

I have found from my psychological studies and personal experiences that there are two very simple questions to help anyone restore healthy boundaries in their life to live a dignified life:

What does this situation negatively represent about yourself? How are you tolerating situations and the behaviors of those around you reinforces your low-worth within you? Those in our lives are a mirror of our own biases, hopes, and fears. *"All anger stems from anger at the self."*

What is your worst fear about saying "no"? Have you ever been left with the thought of you are a bad person because someone's behavior has left you feeling guilty? Well, stop! Challenge that thought by thinking about other situations you have been through. When that happens, the thought that you are a "bad person" falls apart. What matters, in the end, is simple math: people will either *add* or *subtract* to your life.

So, what have you written? The things you write are what you should consider your personal boundaries. When someone ignores something on that list, you should consider it as them crossing boundaries that you have respectively set for yourself. Do not ignore how you feel if this happens, for they are there to tell you what is right from wrong.

Inform others about the boundaries you have set for yourself and be forthcoming with what you will and will not tolerate. When you are assertive with your boundaries, this plays an important part in building a positive self-esteem and allows you many opportunities to reinforce your beliefs, what you cherish, and what you deserve from life.

Do YOU?

Take the time for yourself to establish the things that make you feel good about yourself and about your life as a whole, no matter what it is. Just learn to be aware of how you feel when you go about acting on certain things. For example:

- Are you exhausted by the work you do, but feel thrilled when gardening?
- Are you joyful when reading out loud to your children?
- Do you feel a sense of fulfillment when you write poetry or volunteer in your community?

Once you figure out what makes you feel good about yourself, make those things a priority by implementing them into your every day or weekly schedule. No matter what makes sure you go out and do them! This may mean you have to give up other things to make time for them, but it also means that you may need to re-evaluate your schedule and life more so that you are doing what you honestly enjoy.

To ensure that you are doing these things, there are more than likely going to have to be actions you take to get to those happiness goals, such as saving money to buy supplies to paint, waking up an hour earlier, exercising more, etc.

It is important to realize that you need to do what you need to in order to fulfill your happiness goals. You cannot allow yourself to blame others if you do not fulfill these things. It is time to be a little selfish and fill up your own teapot so that you can fill up the cups of others in your life! This will help you to not only feel better and do better by other people, but it will help you to clear the fog on inconsistent negativity from your life and enable you to truly love yourself and your life once more.

PART III

Chapter 1: Is This for You?

Before we start this adventure, we have to ask, who is this intended for? The short answer is that it is for everyone who wants to make a positive change in their lives. The key word there is "want". This is ultimately a choice. You must establish your own journey as the techniques exemplified in this book are just practices. There is no set number of meditation sessions that will unlock mindfulness. The practice of these techniques only increases the chances of your own self-discovery. Your willingness to find that goal is the only way these practices will be effective.

This may seem confusing or even overwhelming, but it should be celebrated! You have made a choice to better your life. You possess the bravery to examine yourself in your own state. You are already stronger for it. There is value in yourself and your life and you have already made the decision to discover yourself at your most honest, happiest state and to continue to not only endure but thrive in a world made by your own choices. The biggest step is the first one, and that step is already behind you. It is time to breathe a sigh of relief, to feel accomplished. The worst part of your journey is behind you.

Now that you have made the first step, where do you go? Obviously, the answer is your own choice. The practices in this book are merely there to help you along the way. This may or may not be a path that you have previously gone down, so use these techniques to guide you in your own journey. Look at this book as a toolkit. There is nothing in these pages that will assume a role of authority over you. That is the beauty of free will! You are free to explore at your own pace in your own order.

"Often, it's not about becoming a new person, but becoming the person you were meant to be, and already are, but don't know how to be."

— Heath L. Buckmaster, Box of Hair: A Fairy Tale

You have already made the most important step, and that step is the one that separates you from your furthest setbacks. There is already so much distance between where you were and where you are now. It is now possible to look back and accept yourself. Standing where you are now, it is possible to see your own worth. You are not your setbacks, and you are not your failures. In fact, you might be the most interesting person you know!

Chapter 2: Your Toolbox, DBT

The goal of Dialectical Behavior Therapy (DBT) is to separate you from behaviors that are harmful to yourself and others and replace them with meaningful habits. Now that you have taken your first step and have separated yourself from your setbacks, you can go even further and discover what it is that makes you truly happy on your own. Finding that you do not live to continue harmful behaviors but discovering and tailoring habits that will enhance the life that you are choosing to live will fill you with serenity and self-love, and it will be all the more meaningful because they will be your own interests and not the consequences of your setbacks. Honestly, how exciting is it to really discover the real you? Someone that you may have never met or may not have seen in a long time and neither has anyone else, a brand-new person who has been there all along.

The defined objectives of DBT is obviously a little more clinical. It includes Mindfulness, Distress Tolerance, Interpersonal Effectiveness, and Emotion Regulation. How does this relate to you, though? How do these skills fit into your new and exciting life? Remember that the goal of this kind of therapy is not to overtake your life, but to be there alongside it to help you discover what it is that makes you the real you.

Mindfulness is not a skill set, more so a state of being. Mindfulness is being aware of the present, in the present, and not to be overwhelmed by what is going on around you. It is an awesome way to be and reinforces who you are because only you have a mind like yours. Whenever you are using your senses to become directly aware of your present state of being, you are being mindful. Mindfulness is also exercised like a muscle. It is something that we all possess, but few regularly practice. Although that statement may not be true for long. There is a growing interest in meditation and a growing awareness of the importance of remaining mindful in every aspect of life from personal to even business. If you were to practice it, you will discover that the feeling of mindfulness becomes stronger the more you exercise that mental muscle. Focus and personal honesty will become stronger as you develop along this path. It is an exciting tool of self-discovery and one that will be explored upon later in this book.

Distress Tolerance is a measurement. It is your ability to accept distress that cannot be changed. Emotional pain is measured on a different scale altogether from physical pain, but it can be just as, or even more, damaging. The real skill here is learning how to find your own way around the distress and accept what you are unable to change. Practicing mindfulness will help you to separate yourself from distress factors but coming to terms with the reality of these stressful situations will no longer be a roadblock, but a defining challenge that will make you stronger and give you skills for future distress management.

"Grant me the serenity, to accept the things I cannot change; courage to change the things I can; and wisdom to know the difference."

Learning the difference between what you can and cannot control is paramount. Once you have accepted the reality of a stressful situation that you cannot control, you cease to try to change it but begin to find a path to live around or through it. Sometimes, the energy spent trying to change an unchangeable situation is more stressful than the original event! You owe it to yourself to not harm yourself. There are even times when the situation only seems to be so stressful because you have spent all of your energy and effort trying to change it instead of taking a step back and accepting it for what it is. You could even come to realize that the situation is more benign than how you have built it up to be inside your head. Sometimes, you can even find a way to turn it into a positive situation! You will never be able to do any of that if you are too busy stressing about the original situation, though.

Interpersonal Effectiveness will help you to build and maintain important relationships, including the one you have with yourself, as well as help you to define priorities and to arrange them in a sensible manner to live your new life the most effective. The clinical method is through the acronym DEAR MAN:

- **D**escribe the current situations
- **E**xpress your feelings and opinions
- **A**ssert yourself by asking for what you want, or by saying no
- **R**eward the person – let them know what they will get out of it
- **M**indful of objectives without distractions (attack the problem, not the person)
- **A**ppear effective and competent
- **N**egotiate alternative solutions

These are effective and healthy steps for conflict resolution and a great tool to have in mind to keep your communication on track and working towards an agreeable solution.

Respect is a trait valued by everybody in one way or another. Respect is earned and kept and can encourage stronger relationships with the important people in your life. Speaking in a respectful tone will lead you to your interpersonal goals in a way than getting agitated towards that person, situation, or even yourself. Self-respect is the true basis of interpersonal respect. Have you ever heard that you must learn to love yourself before you can love another? This is because you define for yourself, and exemplify to others, what respect means to you. How you treat yourself will set the standard for how others will feel that they can treat you. A person who dresses nice and speaks warmly with peers will garner more respect than a person who shows little care for how they want to be treated. Self-respect is important, and you deserve it! You are already stronger for having taken this journey and your story is one that no one else has. You are worthwhile, interesting, and unique. Taking good care of yourself will tell others that you are a person who warrants respect. Another acronym that is helpful about self-respect is FAST.

- **F**air to myself and others
- No **A**pologies for being alive
- **S**tick to values (do not do anything you will regret later)
- **T**ruthful without excuses or exaggeration

You have heard the Golden Rule; treat others as you would like to be treated yourself. Well, that rule works the other way as well! Treat yourself as you would treat others. You deserve the same respect that you would show to others, so do not count yourself out or make sacrifices that make you feel uncomfortable. Be fair to yourself!

If you find that you apologize unnecessarily, stop it! Sometimes, people will tell you that you apologize too much, which only make you feel uncomfortable. You do not have to apologize for anything that you are not truly sorry for. You occupy the same space as your peers and you deserve the same level of respect.

What are your values? Do you know? In your current stage of rebuilding and discovery, your values may change, or you may discover that you have been violating your own values for a long time. With a renewed respect for yourself and a bright new path ahead of you, you are most likely to find out what is truly important to you. Find your core values and remember that you deserve respect. You do not have to apologize for your values and you do not have to compromise your values. Make your identity known and remember that you are valid.

Once you know who you are, what you value, and the fact that you deserve and possess self-respect, honesty becomes easy. You do not have to fabricate yourself to fit in or hide any unsavory traits that you may think that you possess. Your peers will respect an honest you. Honesty to yourself and others is the pinnacle of freedom. You are who you are and who you are is a strong, healthy, and an interesting person! Half-truths and flat out lies do little more than create stress for everyone involved, including yourself. A person with self-respect does not need to create an identity that they do not own. Breathe and relax because you are you!

Chapter 3: Finding Yourself through Mindfulness

Discovering yourself is exciting! It's a journey that is enviable. We have already defined mindfulness, so the next step is to discover how it is practiced and define what your individual goals are. It is important to remember to constantly ask yourself what you want to find in this book. Your individual goals are the goals of this text. What practitioners of mindfulness usually find is greater fulfillment, a deeper understanding of their selves, positive behavioral changes, and more importantly, less suffering.

As you continue down this path, it is important to remember what your truest intentions are because doubts will surface. Mindfulness will need to be practiced and exercised like a muscle. Minds are messy, prone to wandering, prone to doubt, and everyone examines themselves much harsher than their peers would. In the last chapter, you discovered what your values are and who you are as a person. You discovered that self-respect is worth having. Now, it is time to reinforce what you know about yourself and what you want to explore.

Before we get to the actual practices, it is important to note that the path to mindfulness is not linear. It is a little different for everyone and the only outside guide is a collection of experiences from others. The true guide is yourself. Do not fret. Do not succumb to doubt because you may or may not discover a path differently or find a truth not listed in this book. No one can know you as well as you can. Instead of reveling in the doubt or confusion, be excited! You are the first to discover your exact path and you are the first to find your own unique solutions to your setbacks.

At the same time, you may discover that these goals are even connected! As you discover greater fulfillment, you may connect it to lesser suffering, and from there, you may find that you exhibit better behavior and more success in your relationships. Understand that practicing separateness from your suffering could lead to accepting validation from your own positive thoughts and energy.

The most obvious exercise for practicing mindfulness is meditation. It is important to note that meditation is not passive. It is not simply sitting and relaxing with your eyes closed. It is an active exploration of your mind while providing yourself with the least resistance to your own self-discovery. You may not just drop right into it during your first session. An unpracticed mind has never explored in that way. You may not know how to look inward as your senses and instincts are conditioned to look outward for stimulation.

First, you must separate yourself from your reactions. You must understand what your automatic reactions to a stimulus such as stress and joy are and be aware of yourself at the moment that you act automatically. You are not your feelings. You are not your reactions. Imagine you are on the side of a road watching traffic pass back and forth. Every car is a stimulus, feeling, or reaction. You are separate from them and you must merely make a mental note of it, and then let it pass. Be aware of their existence and acknowledge them, but do not react to them. Eventually, your mind will become more still.

Another example is to imagine your mind like a still pool of water. Every thought and stimulus is a pebble dropped in that pool. Those pebbles create concentric ripples that expand outward, and then even out. If you reach into the water to grab that pebble, you will only create a splash and larger ripples. Eventually, the pebbles will slow, and your quietest realizations and truths will surface. Do not fear! This is your truest self. This is exciting and another great achievement along with your journey to a more peaceful and successful you. After those truths have passed without judgment, your pool of water will fall even more still. You will experience true serenity and discover the most honest definition of a quiet mind. This is peace.

To practice meditation, you must first dedicate time and space to your session. You do not need a special pillow or certain music or any equipment whatsoever, just time and space to practice. Sit in a comfortable position that you will not stress to maintain and close your eyes. Next, just acknowledge the moment as it is. Observe it without judgment or interaction. Just simply be in the moment without exerting effort or energy towards it. Pay attention to the sensations of air passing through your nostrils or the presence of sound in your ears. Let the moment pass through you as you sit peacefully in it. The goal is not simply to be calm, it is to be aware of the moment as it is happening right now without interaction or judgment. The next step is not so much a step, but a reassurance. Judgments will rise. It is inevitable, especially when you are first practicing. Remain calm and remain practicing. Do not succumb to doubt or frustration. Simply make a note of it, and let it pass. This is an excellent practice for learning how to move on from frustration or feelings of grudge in your waking life. If your mind wanders too far off of your initial concentration, keep returning to the sensation of your breath. Focus on the gentle sensation of the in and out of your breathing. Simply be in your awareness.

Meditation is a proven method to reduce stress, increase clarity, and can even positively rearrange your brain chemistry! You will notice your brain will have less chatter in your normal life, and you will be less prone to anxiety. It is a great practice for finding a "third way" around a conflict. It can even open up your creativity and lower your heart rate and blood pressure. As I have mentioned before, it has even begun to appear in modern business practices. Some higher up CEOs have adopted this daily practice to increase their creativity and productivity and reduce their stress level in the fast-paced environment that is business. Everyone from athletes to political figures to your average working man benefits from this simple practice.

If you chose to partake in this particular practice, you are unlikely to regret it.

The next chapter will focus on advanced meditation techniques for when you discover that you like this new calmer, more focused you!

Chapter 4: Taking Mindfulness to the Next Level with Advanced Meditation Techniques

If you have chosen to give meditation a try, then congratulations! You should feel proud of yourself for having the courage to try something new. You should feel reinforced in your feelings of solidity in your new and healthy life. You have made an actual effort and have taken real-life actions! This is another moment to look at just how far you have come. How has meditation affected your life already? Do you feel a renewed clarity? This chapter will show you advanced techniques that you can practice to further expand your meditation practices.

An easy form of meditation that you can incorporate in your daily life is called a Walking Meditation. Obviously, this can be done simply while walking, or any form of ambulation that you use to get around. It is an action that you do naturally and has been for years. You probably learned how to walk before you learned how to read! This kind of easy, almost automatic and steady movement is a perfect environment to study your meditation practices.

First, you must stand up straight. Keep your back straight as you practice this. It is important to find the posture that is comfortable and promotes easy steps and focus. Next, place your hands together just above your belly button with your thumbs curled in towards your palms. This position promotes a comfortable posture that brings your focus to your center. Your arms are not swaying, and you feel self-contained and comfortable. Now, let your gaze drop slightly. This will also allow you to focus while being aware of where you are walking to. Just like with normal sitting meditation, try not to get lost in outside stimuli, just simply make a note of them and continue on with your focus inwards. Now, you are ready to take your first step. In the last section, I mentioned that breathing could be used to bring your focus back to your center.

In this exercise, you will use your steady footfalls to create a rhythmic cadence for you to keep your central focus on. Notice, without interacting, the sensation of the ground on your feet (or whatever mode of transportation that you would use to get around on your own). Notice as the ground rolls from the back to the front of your foot. Notice the gentle bounce of your body as you move along. Now, do the same with the next step and the next. Make sure to walk at a slightly slower pace than usual. It is not necessary to move ridiculously slow, just make sure that it is at a pace where you are able to focus on your gentle and rhythmic movements and still move along at a comfortable speed.

Benefits of this style of meditation are that it allows you to further exercise your focus outside of the room or environment that you have become comfortable meditating in. It allows you to start connecting that focus to your daily life as you practice maintaining that focus during the natural and unpredictable distractions that occur just in a day out. You will also begin to appreciate the seemingly mundane aspects of your day, bringing focus and renewed eyes to aspects of this wonderful life that may have gone unnoticed or underappreciated previously. A cloud moving in front of the sun might bring certain effects to your attention like the changing colors or temperature of this temporary state. You might find a renewed appreciation for the sun and life in general. A gentle breeze might remind you of how temporary forces in your life are. A passing conversation might show you how calm, focused, and centered you are feeling in the moment versus how frantic and anxious the average person is in their daily life. You will discover all of these things while keeping your focus centered. It is important to not react to any of their thoughts, just simply recognize the existence of these thoughts, and let them pass naturally on their own. Bringing your meditation practices from your sterile environment to the waking world is an excellent practice for learning how to maintain and call upon this state of focus when there are events in your life that may be exciting or stressful.

The next technique is quite the opposite. Instead of walking, this technique is most effective while laying down, but it can be done in a sitting position. It is called a Body Scan, and it is used to focus on your physical wellbeing. It gives the sensation of infusing your body with a healing breath.

First, you must sit or lie in a comfortable position. Do not pick a position or surface that will become uncomfortable or distracting during your meditation. Once you are in a good position, place your hands on your stomach in the same manner in which you did during the Walking Meditation, just above your belly button in a comfortable position that brings your focus to the center of your body in a full rest. Once you are in this position, you might find it easier to focus if you close your eyes. Now, take a few deep breaths. Take note of the moment as you are in it, just like you have practiced in the basic meditation technique. Then bring your attention to your body. Notice the sensation and pressure of the floor or chair on your back or legs. Keep taking deep breaths, but this time, notice the invigorating life that fills your body when you inhale deeply and then feel a deeper sense of relaxation on every exhale. Fall deeper and deeper into your focused state with each incremental breath. You may start to notice more minute sensations such as your pulse under your skin, or little hairs standing up on your arm as your body becomes more relaxed and focus.

Now, bring your focus to your stomach area. If your stomach is tense, let it loose. You might even notice that your entire body relaxes as you release the tension in your stomach. Shift your focus from your stomach to your hands just above that area. See if you can allow your hands to soften even more. Feel your body relax even another level. Now, bring your focus to your arms. Let the tension loose in your shoulders. Let the tension loose in your biceps and forearms. After that, it is time to bring your focus to your neck. Let the muscles

119

in your neck relax. It is perfectly acceptable to let your body shift as your muscles become systematically more relaxed. It is almost bound to happen as you are achieving new levels of relaxation. How relaxed you are now will make your initial assessment when you first lied down seem so distant.

After you have relaxed your neck, then it is time to focus on your jaw. Let that tension go. In your waking life, the average person carries extra tension especially in their jaw, shoulders, and fists without even realizing it. You might perceive yourself as relaxed when in actuality; you are much tenser than what is comfortable. This is one of those realizations that you come across through meditation that is an invaluable lesson that you have taught yourself. After you have rolled your relaxing focus over your entire body, take a mental snapshot of your body as a whole. Notice your body in the same way that you notice passing thoughts in the basic meditation technique. You may realize that your body is yours, but it is not you. Your body is a vessel and a tool for who you really are. That separation is important when you practice meditation. It is what allows you to examine thoughts without attachment. Take one more deep breath and allow your eyes to open, feeling a new sense of invigoration and relaxation.

Congratulations! With these three meditation techniques; the basic meditation, the Body Scan, and the Walking Meditation, you are able to perceive and react to thoughts and stimuli within your mind, your body, and your world in a healthy way. There is nothing that you should not be able to process using these techniques. You now have the tools to tackle any hardships along your journey. On top of that, you now have a new perspective that is exciting to explore as you find new hobbies, relationships, and life choices. Now even simple tasks like breathing, walking, or even just existing can be healing and full of positive energy!

The next chapter will focus on processing negative thought patterns in a healthy way. Now that you have this new perspective and new tools, it should be easy to separate yourself from negative thoughts that may surface from your past or present life. Do not fear! You are ready. You are stronger than you have ever been, and you can tackle any setbacks you have experienced, or are currently experiencing. Take a moment to celebrate where you are versus where you have been!

Chapter 5: Using Your New Tools to Process Negative Emotions

Negative emotions will occur. It is the inevitability that comes with the endless possibilities of life. You cannot reasonably expect to live your entire life and never feel sad, hurt, angry, betrayed, embarrassed, or any other emotion that can be perceived as negative. In this chapter, we will review the skills that you have learned to more effectively process your emotions when an inevitably negative emotion occurs. Through Dialectical Behavior Therapy, Emotion Regulation breaks down into three goals.

1. Understand one's emotions
2. Reduce emotional vulnerability
3. Decrease emotional suffering

The first step begins with a simple truth, and that is emotions are not bad. Even negative emotions are not something to just be avoided. It is impossible, and unhealthy to attempt, to avoid every negative emotion that you will come across in your life. Attachment to negative feelings is what causes real suffering. You learned from the last two chapters how to separate yourself from thoughts and emotions. You simply must acknowledge the emotion and/or event, and then let it pass. It is important to acknowledge these emotions, though. Try to define your emotions clearly. Using phrases like "I feel bad" does not give a clear understanding of how you are feeling. Instead of "bad", expand on that. Pinpoint it by saying you feel frustrated, depressed, anxious, or angry. Understanding what and how you are feeling is integral to processing those feelings. It is also important to understand the difference between primary and secondary emotions.

Primary emotions are reactions to an outside stimulus, and secondary emotions are reactions to those primary emotions. For example, if you felt depressed later about being too angry at a friend, then anger would be the primary emotion while depression would be the secondary emotion. The secondary emotion is a judgment of the primary emotion. Learning how to acknowledge emotions without judgment is essential because secondary emotions are destructive. Also, learning how to process negative events without succumbing to negative emotions is very important. Maybe being angry at the friend was not the proper response when you could have used the DEAR MAN acronym in the second chapter of this book to properly resolve that event and those feelings in a way that would solve the issue and be beneficial to both you and your friend. Remember that emotions are not your identity. Emotions are there just to alert you to stimuli that are beneficial or problematic. How you process and express these emotions is entirely up to you.

Reducing emotional vulnerability will increase the stability of your emotions, simply put. In DBT, the methods for reducing emotional vulnerability is through action. It will teach you to create positive habits and experiences to balance out the negative feelings you might be feeling. An easy acronym to remember for this is PLEASE MASTER.

PL – represents taking care of your physical body and reducing or treating illness
E – eat a balanced diet
A – is for avoiding alcohol and drugs, which can only heighten or fabricate negative feelings
S – Sleep. It is important to get regular sleep
E – The last E is for exercise. Much like meditation, it will increase in benefits the more you practice.

MASTER – This one is the fun one. Master positive activities to increase your sense of well-being and accomplishment.

Your health affects your emotional state. This ties into the self-respect section that we talked about in the second chapter. You will feel much better physically and emotionally if you raise your standards of how you treat yourself. Getting regular sleep, exercise, and only treating your body and yourself to healthy food and activities will do absolute wonders for your confidence. This also includes avoiding alcohol and drugs. It is too easy to mask feelings with these substances, and as we have learned, that is not a healthy way to process those emotions. Avoiding emotions, especially with mind-altering substances, does not make those emotions go away. It is not a permanent solution, it only encourages you to chase that perceived temporary safety from those emotions while your body is developing an addiction to the actual substance. It is a trap and can only work to undo all of the work that you have already accomplished. Treat yourself better than that because not only do you have self-respect, but you deserve it.

Now, I am going to circle back to the PL portion of the PLEASE MASTER acronym. After you understand the steps necessary for taking care of your body, you will understand that it is important to monitor your body as a whole. This includes taking care of illnesses when they arrive. Illness is another inevitability of life. Much like emotions, it is important to process them in a healthy manner to avoid further damage. You deserve to live in a healthy body and you owe it to yourself to take care of yourself. Living in a healthy body will give you peace of mind. Knowing that at the end of the day, you are physically feeling healthy will put other situations in perspective and it will be one more positive that you can weigh against negative emotions when they occur. Along with exercise and meditation, you can choose to MASTER other positive activities in your life. Developing or rediscovering a hobby is exciting and can give new meaning and a new sense of accomplishment in your life!

After you have learned these skills, you are ready to learn how to decrease emotional suffering. In DBT, it is comprised of only two skills: Letting go and taking opposite action.

Letting go refers to what we have already learned, by using our mindfulness to process emotions in a healthy way by letting them pass without developing secondary emotions to attach to the primary emotions. Taking opposite action means engaging in actions that are in direct contrast to the negative feelings that you are experiencing. For example, instead of crying when a feeling of depression is acknowledged, try to stand straight, speak confidently, and react to the stimulus or event in a healthy way. This is not to ignore that emotion. It is an exercise to lessen the length and severity of the emotion. It is important to acknowledge emotions, but that does not mean that you have to be subordinate to them. You do not need to let emotions control how you think and act. It can also give you a new perspective on a situation that you may have reacted automatically too.

With these skills, coupled with the skills you have learned in the previous few chapters, you can process emotions internally in your mind, body, and everyday life and also express those emotions after you have processed them. Even more to add to that, you have developed a renewed sense of self-respect through self-care and new or rediscovered hobbies. You are now taking steps to replace negative habits and feelings with positive feelings and activities you enjoy and that are uniquely representative of you! You may start to feel that you are meeting the real you, a more positive and honest version of yourself, doing things that you enjoy.

Chapter 6: Defining Your Goals, Your Values, and Yourself

Now, instead of learning something new, it is time to reassess yourself after what you have already learned. Do you remember those goals and values that you defined for yourself at the beginning of this book? Well much like how we discovered new levels of relaxation during the Body Scan meditation, it is time to discover new levels of yourself. Maybe after you have practiced meditation and studied the different goals of DBT, your renewed sense of self and awareness can further sharpen your goals and expectations from your new life. It is even possible that you have already achieved and mastered some of your goals. If you have, then congratulations! It is time to reassess what is important to you and what you can get out of this book. If you have not achieved any of your goals yet, then do not worry! Hopefully, you have set expectations at a reasonable level and you are mindful of what you are able to achieve within yourself. It is good to have both long-term and short-term goals. It is important, even, to balance both so you are able to celebrate achievements along the path to a life-affirming goal that you may not have been able to achieve without taking that all important first step along this journey.

Each new skill you learn is a skill you would not have had if you would have maintained your negative feelings and habits. There are questions for you now that only you can answer. How is it that you feel? How do you feel in a general sense of wellbeing? How far along do you think you have traveled? You are most likely aware of your progress and it is good to celebrate along the way. These steps you are taking are not steps that any one person could take for you, no matter how influential or qualified. Just like how meditation and mindfulness is a study of you, the steps you have taken are entirely unique to you.

Having said all of that, it is important to allow positive feelings to be acknowledged and witnessed. Many have a hard time accepting themselves in their own achievements. Judgments upon oneself can absolutely be the harshest. It is easy for faults and negative feelings to seem large and overwhelming when you are standing so near to them. These negative feelings cause you to stress and can be impossible to simply ignore. This is why we learn to process those feelings and resolve them instead of trying in vain to ignore them. An unresolved negative feeling can trigger a survival response, which is why it is impossible to ignore said feelings. In this way, unresolved negative feelings make it near impossible to accept positive feelings about yourself.

Your body does not feel the need to react to positive feelings because it feels that the situation is resolved because it ended on a satisfying conclusion. Your body will tell you that your time and effort need to be spent resolving those negative feelings because they are triggering a survival response in you. Now that you have learned how to bring negative feelings to a positive and productive conclusion, it is now possible to accept your positive traits and individuality. It is even possible to meet yourself without those impossible stresses in your life. How exciting and life-affirming is that! How much better off are you now in relation to how you were before you took this journey?

Now, that you know your goals, and you know yourself, what are your values in your new life now? What have you learned that you could possibly maintain, or even teach others? Maybe you recognize the work that you have put in and are starting to recognize the results of hard work. Maybe you value patience and understanding because practicing meditation has taught you how to discover feelings that were always there, just buried. All this book can do is speculate and give examples to what you may be feeling. It is your unique journey that is your real teacher. You have taught yourself how to heal. You have taught yourself how to take the first step, and you have taught yourself how to recognize greatness within yourself.

Are there people in your life who would be proud of you for where you are now? If so, you should greet them and share your renewed sense of pride and clarity with them. It is reaffirming of your own sense of accomplishments to have it validated by those you love, those you admire, and those you respect. Sometimes, it can give a new perspective to emphasize with someone else and share a joyful feeling with them. You are no longer in a cave of your own misjudgments, both internal and external. You have established yourself out in the light. You can walk among the world with your head high instead of living in the past and inside of your own head. You see the world for how it actually is and not through the lens of prior transgressions or feelings of worthlessness. It is even possible to look back at how you used to exist and treat yourself and separate yourself enough from it that you can even brush it off. That is not you anymore. You are the real you now. You are the you that you were meant to be, a much happier and more honest you who recognizes real emotions instead of perceived injustices to yourself.

Chapter 7: Living in the Positive!

Now that you have created a positive atmosphere for your mind to exist in, you are probably feeling a new motivation and longing to explore the world in your new self. What do you do with all of this motivation? It is important to put this good energy to use as to not fall back into negative habits that your old self has come to reinforce. You are at a crucial step where you should give great importance to channeling this positive energy into positive habits.

Something that you can do for yourself is to continue to practice meditation and exercise. Your new positive life starts at your core. Your core being yourself. You have learned a renewed sense of self-respect and discovered some deep insight into yourself. Now, it is time to maintain it. You can continue to live positive as long as you take care of yourself. Imagine yourself in a fancy car. It can look nice on the outside, but if the engine is not kept in good condition, it will not function as intended. Every new positive action starts with a sense of wellbeing.

Other ways to maintain your emotional stability through practice is to find a creative outlet for your feelings. If you feel that you are the creative type of person, then you may already have some of these hobbies. You may even have hobbies that you have not visited in a long time. Picking up an old hobby can help you connect with who you were before you found yourself down a darker path. It can give you a sense that you are picking up where you left off and reassure you that this you is the real you. If you are not a creative person or have not found an interest in a hobby, then do not worry! Another way that you can strengthen your mental focus and reinforce this new positive you are to learn. Reading is a proven method to increase cognitive faculties and helps you to directly discover interesting perspectives that you may not have come to on your own independently. Maybe, you will even discover ways to learn about aspects of your life that you have put on hold. Projects and promises made to others and you can now be fulfilled because you are now breathing easy and have a new motivation for life.

Great! Now that you have a healthy and positive sense of wellbeing, you can further reinforce your new positive life by engaging in productive social activities. Before I get into examples of this, I want to further explore the benefits.

Giving back to your community outwardly shows that you want to be engaged with society. You recognize yourself as a part of a whole and you are devoid of an ego that alienates you from your peers. It is not a struggle for your individuality though; you have already explored and defined yourself to yourself. Now, it is time to show who you are to the world! A person who lives inside of their own negative thought patterns does not want to be a part of society. They will build their own mental walls to keep themselves from embarrassment, anger, shame, or any other negative thought patterns associated with social interaction. Maybe they feel that society owes them something. An overinflated ego is another trepidation to avoid. Now that you are free of all of these negative thought patterns, you can enjoy social interaction with a head held high and nothing to apologize for. Another key benefit that you may not have seen or realized before, is that doing something nice for others simply feels good. You are able to emphasize the happiness of others. Seeing a smile on another person's face that you have caused can feel so rewarding in ways that you have never felt before! Even for more selfish reasons, it feels good, as in the sense of being the hero of someone's day. It is a wholesome feeling. It is a feeling that is entirely guilt-free.

Some examples of positive social outings would be simple activities like volunteer work or attending or even participating in sports events. Maybe your place of employment has a softball league, or your colleagues enjoy disc golf.

These are activities that directly give back to your community or peer group. These are higher levels of commitment, so if you are not ready for that quite yet, maybe you could try something a little less structured. Meeting trusted friends in a relaxed social environment could be a little bit more comfortable for you. Invite a friend, or a few friends, out for lunch or to a store of your common interests. This kind of setting makes for a good conversation that is not so personal if you are not ready for that. It is perfectly acceptable to take your time developing your social identity, as this step is very important. Meeting friends in this kind of setting can also help you learn more about your friends and even yourself! Maybe they have an interest that you did not even know that you had! Maybe you have a friend who is very interested in tabletop gaming, which might be an area of interest that you have never explored! Your friends and new interests will most likely lead you to new friends and even more positive and interesting activities. It is easy to get sucked into the positive life; all you have to do is take the first step!

Working within your comfortable level of commitment is essential, but it is also important to actually engage in these or similar activities. The goal of this section is to establish new positive habits to replace self-destructive habits. Just like how picking up and reading this book was a crucial first step, this is another crucial step. Do not fret though! This step is easier than what you would think. Most of the time, the fear associated with the activity is much worse than the actual activity, and you should know how to properly process negative thought patterns. All you have to do is breathe and take that step. Your friends, family, and colleagues will be more than happy to have you included.

It is important to establish positive relationships that engage in positive activities. It is also important to allow yourself to learn what positive social activities are. A common misconception, reinforced by advertisements and common television shows, is that all social activity takes place with alcohol. That is simply not true. In fact, the most productive and happiest people may rarely step foot in one of these establishments. As a side note, you may also be surprised at the money you save when you do not frequently visit these establishments, which brings me back to advertisements. That is why those media outlets pursue that lifestyle; it is purely to promote a lifestyle that will earn their company more money. In that respect, establish your own idea of happiness! Find out what it is that truly makes you happy! You are most likely to find that engaging with friends develops real bonds and promotes honest happiness. You are most likely to find that volunteer work, or even saying yes when someone asks for a favor, is more fulfilling than anything that you have experienced in your previous life.

You should feel proud of yourself for taking this step! Now that you are taking steps to not only better yourself, but to solidify and reinforce it with positive social activities, there is nothing that can get in your way on your path to being happier, more wholesome you! Once again, congratulations!

Chapter 8: How DBT Has Enhanced Your Life

Although this book has seemed to have an almost conversational flow, it has actually followed very closely to the five functions of DBT. As this book has mentioned before, the goal of this is not to assume an authoritative role over you, the reader. This book was designed to reinforce your own choices and merely give examples of positive living for those who may be unaware or fearful of how to live as such. Having said that, it is now time to relate what we have learned to the five functions of Dialectical Behavior Therapy. Before we do that, let's define what those five functions are.

- Enhance client's capabilities
- Improve the client's motivation
- Assure generalization to the client's natural environment
- Structure the environment
- Enhance the therapist's capabilities and support their motivation

The clinical way to go about enhancing your capabilities is to reinforce the skills of DBT. We have used many skills directly from the actual standard of DBT, such as the acronyms DEAR MAN, FAST, and PLEASE MASTER. These are acronyms that you would become familiar with if you were to attend a regular DBT session. We have also discussed important skills like practicing mindfulness and emotional regulation. These are also skills that you are most likely to encounter in an actual DBT session. This book has taken those lessons and broken them down for you to study, practice, and make into your own at your own pace by your own choices. Using these skills in your own life will only work to enhance the quality of your life and introduce you to lifestyles that mirror your interests, even those that you may not be aware that you have. This is an exciting time to be alive, and an exciting time for you!

The next function of DBT is the enhancement of the client's motivation. This book was designed to keep you motivated throughout, but it is not what was written or the speed in which you read it. The real motivation comes from you. You have rewarded yourself for picking up this book and sticking to it all the way to the end. By now, you deserve to have developed a sense of pride in making these positive changes in your life! There is no outside force that can motivate you to the extent that you can motivate yourself.

This book was written to be a companion to your own life. You are free to read or not read, follow or not follow, at your own pace. The fact that you have made it this far is something to be celebrated. It shows that you are honest in your desire to rid yourself of negative thought processes and self-destructive habits. There is not a single person or entity that is able to instill that level of motivation inside of you. You have shown that you are committed; not to this book or these processes, but you are committed to yourself. You have already taken better care of yourself than previously you might have thought possible. It is not only acceptable but appropriate to celebrate yourself at this time. This is a real achievement that you have accomplished, and one that many people take multiple tries to achieve. Some may not ever get to the level of clarity and health that you have already achieved for yourself. Once again, Congratulations!

The third function of DBT may seem confusing at first. It is to assure generalization to the client's natural environment. What that means is that this treatment, and this book, is designed to be a companion piece to live alongside without overtaking your life. This is not a program designed to put your life on hold. The effectiveness of this is that it promotes ease of transition into your new lifestyle while giving examples that are digestible by you because they relate to you, just as you are. It is easy to take this book with you and read it at your own pace or use the skills you have learned through a DBT session or in this book while you go about living your day-to-day life. There is no commitment besides the commitment that you have made to yourself and are comfortable with.

In an actual DBT session, they would address this function within the moment coaching. You would have access to a 24/7 phone number that you would be encouraged to call if you are having a hard time with applying the lessons to your life you would have learned during a session. This is an excellent tool, and if you were to attend a DBT session, I would strongly encourage you to feel free to use it. These coaches are not there to judge your choices. They understand the material and are also encouraged to process emotions without judgment. This is purely for the benefit of you! It is also encouraging to have outside motivation when your motivation might be hitting a low point. There is nothing to worry about though, just like the inevitability of sickness or negative thoughts, you cannot fault yourself for when your motivation is feeling weaker at the moment. Just relax, call that number, and celebrate yourself for making the positive choice at that moment when you may not have previously.

We are almost through the list here, I hope that you feel encouraged to continue. The fourth function of DBT is to structure the client's environment. This one can seem almost scary because you have gone this far along your own choices. There is nothing to fear though because this step is not designed to take away your choices, merely to help you and provide tools for you to make positive choices when you may not have previously. How a DBT session would go about doing that would be to assign you a case manager. This is someone who is dedicated to your case and is working with you to ensure your success.

An important aspect of this function is the thought process when accepting it. It is not there to control your lifestyle. When a client has made poor life choices and made a habit out of them, then they might not be aware of or be comfortable with lifestyle choices that are more positive and sustainable. You have already decided to live a positive life, now it is time to learn how. That is the purpose of this function. In DBT, there is a strong focus on replacing negative habits with more positive habits. This is because pure motivation has to be outwardly expressed and used for it to continue. Imagine your positive motivation as a match. You can light the match, and it will burn for a while. It is hot, it is bright. It has the potential to continue on, but it can only continue on if fuel is introduced to the match. Imagine this function of DBT as a pile of wood arranged for you in a fire pit, ready to be lit by your motivational match. Once you apply the match to the wood in the fire pit, then the fire burns much longer in a safe environment. Your motivation must be applied to a positive atmosphere to continue on. Your case manager or other individuals in your DBT session use this function to safely provide you with those structured, positive environments. Go forth and do well for yourself and others!

Have you made it this far? I hope that you have because this is now the final function of Dialectical Behavior Therapy. That function is to enhance the therapist's capabilities and support their motivation. DBT therapists work in a team to more effectively enhance the lives and understanding of their clients. This is important for the team as well as the client. A typical DBT team meeting may start with a mindfulness exercise, reading of the previous minutes, and then discuss strategies to further their treatment. It is important for you to be engaging and helpful along with your therapist as this whole treatment only works with your commitment. An example of this would be to imagine you and your therapist on a rowboat. Your therapist will not be able to motivate you to continue to row if they are not participating in the work. Your therapist can also not row by themselves if you are not helping. This whole style of treatment is designed to be a cooperative endeavor. You should feel excited and encouraged to participate. The end result will be a happier, more positive you!

This chapter is here to serve the purpose of relating what you have learned to the structured skills that are discussed in an actual Dialectical Behavior Therapy session. It is strongly encouraged that you attend these sessions and take what you have learned in this book with you to those sessions. There is nothing that you should not be able to achieve in this aspect of your life between this book, those sessions, and your own motivation! You have a threefold angle of attack on your negative habits that you wish to eradicate from your life. Finding a DBT session is easy, as it is a growing style of treatment. Everyone involved wishes only the best of success for you! Continue on with your own choices and feel proud of how far you have come!

PART IV

Chapter 1: Back to the Basics

When most people think of mindfulness, they envision monks or yogis, sitting cross legged for hours with closed eyes and poised fingers overlooking the Himalayas. Although mindfulness is present in the lives of monks and yogis, what most people don't know is how easy it is to incorporate mindfulness into our everyday lives. As a matter of fact, a mindful state is the most natural and restful state for human beings—a state in which we were all living and moving in as children. If you think back to your childhood, you will likely remember that your concept of time and perception of reality was much different. Most children are very in touch with their emotions, letting them come and go naturally. If a child falls down in one moment and skins their knee, the child will likely begin to cry. However, if a few moments later they are being offered ice cream, their tears will dry, and they will continue on with their day. Mindfulness is the reason children are so in tune with the details of life that adults seem to miss. It is also the reason they are more likely to screech with joy, run around excitedly in enjoyable environments, wake up easily in the morning, and take the time they need to calm down from anger or sadness until the next happy moment arises. Children spend very little time thinking about things beyond the present moment. Even if they have something to look forward to, they are still likely to become invested in the moment at hand, whether that is playing, enjoying time with their parents, or eating a meal. So, what happens as people grow older that brings us away from this natural state of mindfulness?

There are a number of factors that pull people out of the present moment. From the time a child begins elementary school, they are presented with a schedule for the day, which remains relatively the same. Children are expected to remain within the structures presented to them, and the idea of forward-thinking and preparing for the next hour's activity becomes introduced. As they grow, children will likely have more expectations placed upon them, whether those expectations are academic, extracurricular, or within the home. Of course, it is necessary for children to learn how to be responsible and dedicate the time they need to the important things in life. However, as they become further exposed to the constant rush and future-oriented thinking of their parents and teachers, they come to see time as something that no longer belongs to them to fully inhabit.

Furthermore, as people approach teenage and young adulthood, they will begin to face challenges that most children are either shielded from or otherwise unaware of. People become flooded with the pressure to perform well and always be doing more today than yesterday. Although the expectations of cultures and societies vary, we can be sure that people are overwhelmed with the pressure to meet those expectations in order to be considered successful and valid. Once one bar is crossed, another one is waiting, and there is no time to slack. Additionally, the older people become, the more likely they are to be subject to long-lasting pain in their lives. This can come in the form of relationships ending, failing to accomplish something, being mistreated by other people, losing and grieving loved ones, or coming to terms with painful childhood events that did not make sense at the time. Teenagers become increasingly subject to mental health issues as they advance into adulthood, having to face all of the hard realities of the world and still come out on top. People may also be subject to trauma as a result of illness, accident, or abuse. All of these factors are enough to work against people and pull them out of the present moment, either because it is too painful to be there, or because they are simply too distracted.

Human beings experience over 60,000 thoughts per day, but the vast majority are dedicated either to planning for the future or worrying about the past. Becoming overly concerned about the future or steeping in the pains or regrets of the past can increase levels of stress in the body, which makes people more anxious and prone to physical health problems.

The mind naturally wanders, and it is impossible to keep thoughts from coming. Mindfulness is not a tool to eradicate such thoughts, as is the common misconception. Rather, it is a tool through which to acknowledge the thoughts the mind creates, bring attention to them, and allow them to move through. This ultimately brings people into what is happening here and now and gives them more control over their minds and how they orient themselves in their environments.

Because mindfulness is a skill that all human beings are equipped with at our core, it is something that can be re-learned. Just as we exercise our bodies to strengthen our muscles, so we must work to strengthen our brain through mindfulness. The way this strengthening happens is through being aware of thoughts as they arise, then breathing back into the present moment. The more practice is given to returning to the present moment, the stronger the mind will become in remaining in the present more often. Just as the body physically strengthens and becomes healthier over time with exercise, mindfulness exercises can physically change the structure of the brain to make it healthier. Mindfulness activates the positive components of the hippocampus, which is the part of the brain responsible for good things like creativity, joy, and the ability to process emotions. This, in turn, decreases stress levels, depressive tendencies, addictive behaviors, and the fight or flight instinct by shrinking the part of the brain responsible for negative things (the amygdala). Overall, increased mindfulness is the key to a longer, healthier, more creative, and more joyful life.

Chapter 2: Unlocking Your True Purpose Through Mindfulness

Re-centering Yourself

Everyone has days where everything seems to be spinning out of control, and there seems to be no way to manage the chaos. The days where you wake up late, run late to work, spill coffee on your shirt, get cut off on the road, get yelled at by your boss, spend the entire day at work in a confused frenzy, only to come home and bicker with your partner. Since the beginning of time, the human mind has been conditioned to release stress hormones and illicit the fight or flight instinct for the purpose of protection and survival. In the past, this primal instinct was very useful for escaping threats. As times have changed, the threats have become less severe, but the brain's response has remained largely the same. Now, these fight or flight reactions are likely to be triggered by everyday scenarios, such as those previously detailed. The hormone-induced responses that occur when we're stressed out are quick to send us spiraling into emotionally dramatic, and far less peaceful dimensions.

The good news is, mindfulness can be used as a tool for re-centering and gaining control over your anxiety and emotional reactions when you start to feel yourself spiral. Although there is no way to avoid stress and drama in daily life, mindfulness can serve as a shield of calm presence to protect your well-being. If you are preparing to enter a situation that you anticipate could be stressful, like a high-stakes day at work, a scary doctor's appointment, or a difficult conversation with a loved one, it can be incredibly helpful to bring yourself down to a more calm and balanced state in preparation for the stress you are about to deal with. You may find yourself with a racing heart, sweating palms, an unclear head, and the feeling of "butterflies in your stomach." Another area where it is common to feel these physical effects of anxiety is when encountering dramatic situations. Drama can arise tense moments with other people, as well as within the theoretical situations people create for themselves when worrying about what they cannot control (for example, the perception other people have of them, or events that may or may not occur in the future). Giving attention to what is happening in your mind and body and allowing yourself to breathe into the moment can be a total lifesaver in moments of drama or stress. Two to three minutes of deep breathing in your car before going to work, or taking a few deep breaths before reacting in a tense moment, can make a drastic difference in your sense of balance and your ability to deal with stress without launching into fight or flight.

Giving Your Emotions Space

The goal of mindfulness is not to eliminate emotions, but rather, to gain control over the impact they have on how we orient ourselves in the world. It is vital to honor our emotions and give them space to exist and teach us, without letting them seize control. Mindfulness is an excellent tool for giving our emotions space in this way. When an emotion arises, mindfulness gives us a chance to observe that emotion without judgment. In this calm space, we can ask our emotions, "What are you trying to teach me?" We can more clearly discern why we are experiencing a certain emotion, and become in touch with the deeper needs that may have caused that emotion to arise. Just as a child may cry when they need to be nourished our held, we may find ourselves growing angry or agitated when we need support, touch, or self-care. Similarly, we may find ourselves feeling stressed or anxious in scenarios that are subconsciously triggering moments from the past. In these cases, our stress and anxiety are begging us to become in touch with our past self, reminding ourselves that we are safe, and the traumatic moments from the past are over. Once our emotions have been given a non-judgmental space to exist, they can smoothly and peacefully move through the body and be released. This frees us to move from moment to moment like children do, without being constrained by unresolved emotions. Additionally, giving this space to our emotions in mindfulness helps to temper our reactions, which can prevent us from acting out in extreme ways and potentially doing or saying something we regret.

Making Clear Decisions

With the human mind constantly being muddled with thoughts, it can be hard to see things clearly. Sometimes our minds are cluttered by the expectations flying at us from every different direction, or perhaps by our fears of what will happen if things don't go to plan. When it comes to making decisions, we are often faced with numerous options, and it can be difficult to navigate through the chaos in our minds to come to a well thought out resolution. In a distracted, anxious, or removed state, our minds are like a pond on a rainy day—rippling to a point where there is no more clarity. Mindfulness is the calming of the waters, which brings us to a place where we can more clearly think of all possible outcomes of a decision and check in with what we truly need before moving into the next moment.

Keeping Yourself Safe

Although fight or flight instincts originally developed as a way to keep humans safe, in many modern-day scenarios, they do quite the opposite. Let's go back to the example from the beginning of the chapter about the chain of events in a typical chaotic day. If you wake up late in the morning and rush to make your coffee, not paying attention to what you are doing, you run the risk of haphazardly screwing the lid on your to-go cup, then sloshing boiling hot coffee over the edge of the cup and onto yourself as you bolt out the door. Although such a scenario could simply result in a stained shirt, the inattentiveness could have a more drastic effect, such as burning yourself or someone else. Driving to work in a state of panic over running late causes you to be more likely to break the rules of the road— driving too fast, making dangerous decisions when changing lanes, taking turns too fast, running yellow lights just before they turn red, etc. Additionally, the panicked state can lead to anger with yourself or others on the road, which can further impair judgment and put you at greater risk of an accident. Attempting to have a conversation with your boss if you are in fight or flight mode could result in being overly emotional and saying or doing something extreme which could place you at odds within your workplace, potentially even costing your position. Going throughout your day in a frenzy causes you to be less aware of what is going on around you, which can lead to further threats to safety like leaving a burner on, forgetting to eat or drink enough water, or neglecting those in your care (such as pets or children) as a result of your own inner distractions. Finally, as stress from the day carries into the home at the end of the day, it can pose a major threat to relationships. The more stressed out and less clear thinking you are, the more likely you are to say or do something threatening to your partner, to put yourself in an aggressive and volatile situation, and to make brash decisions that have the potential to haunt your future.

Improving Relationships

Just as we must give ourselves space to learn, grow, and process our experiences, we must give that space to those around us as well. When a partner or friend is acting in a way we don't enjoy, mindfulness can allow us to take a step back and look at the situation from a position of empathy. We can allow ourselves to hold space for whatever that person may be going through individually and express our support while also maintaining boundaries and staying in control of what we can. Everyone is deserving of space to be listened to, understood, and supported for who they are. However, it is incredibly difficult to give that space to anyone if it has not been cleared within oneself.

When we operate out of a mindless state, there is hardly any space to meet our own needs and process our own experience, much less to provide that to other people. This can lead us to be closed off to the ones we love, push them away, or act out in anger, selfishness, or aggression. If we have not given space to what is going on within us, we cannot offer full empathy to others. Only 20% of the population is recorded to practice true empathy, which can be linked to the rarity of true mindfulness among adults. Mindfulness allows us to be more present to our own needs in order to hold adequate space for the needs of others as well.

Attention and mutual respect are core elements of every functional relationship. Practicing mindfulness can improve relationships with all the people in our lives by preparing us for every engagement and calming our minds enough to be fully present in the moments we share with others. Mindfulness clears the space for us to listen intentionally to other people and pay more attention to what kind of people they are and what kind of support they need. It allows us to love other people better by increasing our awareness of how they feel most loved. By being present in the moment at hand, as opposed to trapped in the past or future, you are more likely to remember to pick up the phone and give your grandmother a call, to be fully engaged when interacting with your child, or to remember the kind of kombucha your significant other likes best from the store. Not only does mindfulness allow for more meaningful conversations and joyful memories, but it also increases the functionality of our relationships overall so that both ourselves and those we love are feeling fully respected, listened to, and encouraged.

Fostering True Joy

We often hear the term "childlike joy" to describe moments of pure bliss, enthusiasm, and full satisfaction. As people grow into adults, such moments tend to be few and far between, with many remembering the most joyful moments to have been those that occurred in childhood. The expectations of daily life become too much, and most people find themselves trapped in a cycle of constant anticipation. People spend so much time thinking about where they would rather be (on vacation, in bed, enjoying the weekend) that the days melt into each other without us realizing all the moments of our lives we are missing. The biggest societal misconception is that true happiness lies in what we do not yet have. We are flooded with lies such as "Once I can buy this new TV, then I'll be happy," or, "Once I have a partner, then I'll be happy," or, "I'll be happy once I can say I've been to five different countries." Mindfulness abolishes these lies by proving to us that the capacity for true joy lies not in the future but in the here and now. Wherever you are right now, whatever you have, and whichever stage of life you're in, mindfulness reminds you that *this* is your chance to experience beauty and satisfaction like never before. Take time to look at the flowers you did not notice growing in front of your neighbor's house, the complexity of coffee's flavor as it slides down your throat, the way your loved one's eyes crinkle when they smile, the laughter of a child, every intricate flavor of dinner, or the unique people wandering up and down the streets you drive every day to work. It is here that joy resides; all you have to do is be present enough to recognize it.

Chapter 3: Moving Mindfully in Daily Life

Coming to the Present Moment: Daily Guided Mindfulness Meditation With Journaling (Week 1)

Cultivating Mindfulness

This meditation should be done in a space where you feel fully comfortable, safe, and relaxed. Perhaps it is in a corner of your bedroom, in a garden, by your favorite lake, or even in your car. Make sure you can fully relax and avoid distractions. Some people meditate best with instrumental music or nature sounds in the background, while others prefer silence. Feel free to try multiple methods and see which is most soothing to you (this can vary depending on the day). You may do this meditation sitting in a chair, on a mat, or lying flat on your back with your palms up to the sky. You will need to give yourself 5-20 minutes of time to practice, depending on your skill level and current state. If you like, you can set a timer.

Start by coming into the moment with a few deep breaths. Settle into your body and take note of any sensations you feel. If you feel pain, tingling, warmth, or tightness in any part of your body, focus your breath into that space. Imagine any tension unfurling into openness. Notice as your thoughts arise. Take notice of them, then allow them to pass as you come back to the breath. If it is helpful, you can try a breathing pattern in order to culminate focus. To do the 4-4-4 breathing pattern, breathe in for 4 counts, hold for 4 counts, and breathe out for 4 counts. To do the 5-5-7 breathing pattern, breath in for 5 counts, hold for 5 counts, release for 7 counts. Sometimes it helps to imagine breathing in the things you wish to see more of in your daily life (creativity, love, patience, openness) and exhale the negative things (fear, negativity, sadness, stress). Allow yourself to spend a few moments in a more active state of breathing in, releasing, and paying attention to your body.

With practice, you may enter a state where your thoughts slow and you become fully grounded in the present moment. In this state, you are no longer bombarded with thoughts, nor distracted by elements of your environment. It becomes easier to return to the breath. All restlessness and tension in the body seem to melt away, and the mind reaches a flowing, liquified state. There may be days when you cannot enter into this state, and you remain restless throughout the course of the meditation. If this happens, allow it to be that way, observing every thought that arises, then letting it go.

After the time is up, begin to arrive in the moment by moving your body slightly—wiggling your fingers and toes, tensing and releasing your muscles, etc. Next, you're your eyes. Notice how bright and clear the world looks to mindful eyes. Notice the calm, transcendent feeling in your body, and continue to move with it as you go about your day.

Mindfulness Meditation Journal Prompt (Week 1):

What did you feel in your body before beginning? What do you feel now?

Which thoughts continued to arise in your consciousness? Could these thoughts have been trying to teach you something or speak to a deeper need you may have?

How does the world look after opening your eyes? What do you notice?

Come back after going about your day for several hours. Did you bring mindfulness with you into the world? If so, how?

Coming to the Present Moment: Daily Guided Mindfulness Meditation With Journaling (Week 2)

Taking Mindfulness Into the World

This meditation will be done with your eyes open in moments if your daily life. This is not a specific meditation you have to set aside time for, but rather a state you come into. Notice where your attention goes in a given moment. If your attention is drawn to a particular sight, like the nearest tree or a view from the top of a mountain, allow yourself to see it fully. Repeatedly tell yourself, "see, see, see." Breathe as you allow your eyes to truly become totally focused and take in the image fully, allowing it to become a part of your awareness.

If your attention is drawn to an auditory experience, such as the sound of cars on a city street, a rushing body of water, or an internal monologue, give full attention to that thing. Soak in that auditory experience, breathing slowly and telling yourself, "hear, hear, hear."

You may also be drawn to a particular physical or emotional experience within the body. This experience may be positive, like a pleasant bodily sensation or a feeling of joy. It may also be negative, like physical pain, or feelings of anger or feel. Either way, allow yourself to become fully present with what is there, breathing into the experience and seeing what it has to teach you. Breathe into that bodily experience, telling yourself, "feel, feel, feel."

Throughout the day, you'll find that your attention is pulled in various directions. Mindfulness is the choice to tune in to whichever place you're going in a given moment and give full attention to that experience for whatever it is.

Mindfulness Meditation Journal Prompt (Week 2):

How difficult was it to bring mindfulness into your daily life in this way? Where did you face the most challenges?

Did your attention tend towards certain experiences (visual, auditory, bodily) more than others?

Describe a specific moment where you brought mindfulness to your experience and felt truly present. What did you observe?

Coming to the Present Moment: Daily Guided Mindfulness Meditation With Journaling (Week 3)

Mindfulness at Work (or School)

The first part of this meditation should happen in a place outside of work, where you feel safe, calm, and separated from the issues you may face in the workplace. Start by identifying your biggest struggles at work. The journal portion will give you a space to write them down. Do you struggle with productivity? Boredom? Stress? Conflict resolution? Work relationships? Once you have identified your most significant area(s) of struggle, close your eyes and visualize what that unpleasant experience looks like. Perhaps it looks like you, rushing around mindlessly like a bee in a hive, stressed out and too overbooked to step away and breathe because there are more calls to make, more e-mails to send, more things to do. Or, perhaps it is the co-worker, professor, or boss that makes your stomach drop whenever you think about having to interact with them. Perhaps you feel unfulfilled at work and find yourself constantly checking the clock, thinking about the moment you get to leave. Maybe you have so many things to do and no idea where to start, so you waste a lot of time on mindless tasks. Whatever your struggles at work are, use your time and space away from work to safely visualize the situation. Breathe into the mental circumstance.

As you breathe, begin to envision what this experience would look like if it went the way you want it to. Perhaps it looks like the mental clarity that allows you to know exactly what needs to get done and how to make the best possible use of your time. It could be a greater sense of calm and courage when talking with your difficult boss or co-worker and having your message be well-received on their end. It may also be a deeper sense of satisfaction and enjoyment in the work you're doing, providing you the ability to step back and feel a sense of joy with where you're at, without constantly thinking about the next thing. Reframe the moment in your mind until you've created a mental space that feels good. Let yourself sit there, breathing, soaking it in for several minutes.

Once you go into the workplace (or school), you can bring this meditation into your life by going back to the peaceful mental image you've created over and over again. When you begin to feel stressed, bored, anxious, or unproductive, return to the space where you do not feel those things. Bring that energy into your daily work life, and watch how it revolutionizes your experience.

Mindfulness Meditation Journal Prompt (Week 3):

What do you identify as your biggest challenge(s) at work or school?

How does it look when you reframe your struggles to create a positive mental image?

.

What do you observe about bringing this positive mental image into difficult situations in the workplace or at school?

Mini Meditation Toolbox: 15 Quick and Easy Meditations to Integrate Mindfulness Into Your Daily Life

One-Minute Mindfulness

- Find a space where you can be alone, like on your bathroom break or in your car right before going into work, school, or home at the end of the day.

- Set a timer for one minute

- Close your eyes and focus exclusively on your breathing

- Take notice of the stresses, thoughts, and anxieties that arise, then let them go

- When you open your eyes, notice how you feel de-stressed, clear-minded, and prepared to go about your upcoming tasks and interactions with others

5-Minute Body Scan

- Set a timer for 5 minutes (if needed)

- Close your eyes and take several deep, cleansing breaths. You may use the 4-4-4 or 5-5-7 breathing patterns to deepen the breath

- Begin to bring attention to your body

- Take notice of any sensations that arise-- warmth, tingling, tension, etc.

- Bring your attention to the soles of the feet. Tighten your muscles by curling your toes, then release. What sensations do you feel?

- Continue moving up the body to your calves, hips, abdomen, chest, hands, arms, face, and neck. Observe any sensations that arise, and breathe into those sensations.
- Tighten and release the muscles in each of these areas, allowing any pent-up energy or resistance to be released
- Feel your body become grounded, relaxing completely into the floor, bed, or chair as you come into the present moment in your body and all tension melts away

Mindful Bath/Shower (10-minute meditation)

- As you begin your bath or shower, take a moment to breathe. Remove yourself from the stresses of the day and allow yourself to re-center
- Bring attention to each part of your body as you wash it
- Take notice of any sensations you feel as you move from the soles of your feet to the ends of your hair
- Breathe in the pleasant scent of the soaps and the warmth of the water. Allow yourself to feel clean, warm, and safe.
- As you wash each part of your body, thank it for what it does for you. Then, thank yourself for taking care of your body.

Mindful Morning Routine (15-30 minutes)

- Before getting out of bed, begin to stretch gently, letting thoughts come and go as your mind and body wake up. Do not rush yourself.

- Once you are ready to get out of bed, bring your attention to the space around you and the day ahead. Feel yourself become fully present in that space and prepared to move mindfully through your day

- Pay attention to every move you make, from putting on clothes, to washing your face, to setting the water on the stove to boil.

- Cultivate your awareness for the day ahead by moving slowly and calmly, one task at a time, becoming fully awake to the world

Mindful Housekeeping

- Allow yourself to become focused on the task at hand and only that task. Let every other thing you have to do or think about fade into the background.

- Bring your attention to the breath and the specific way your body moves as you complete a particular task or chore

- Give space to any thoughts or emotions that arise in your consciousness, allowing yourself to process them in a mindful state

Mindful Sit-and-Drink (10-minute meditation)

- Find a calm, quiet space where you can sit and observe the world around you (preferably outside or near a window looking outside)
- Pour a glass of your favorite tea, coffee, or cocktail to enjoy
- Eliminate all distractions. Draw your attention to the intricate flavors of the drink, and the pleasure of pulling something you enjoy into your body
- Take notice of the things happening around you. Find the things in the environment that bring you the most peace, and allow their presence with you to help you calm your mind. Become completely indulged in the moment.

Mindful Scheduling (10-minute meditation)

- Sit down with a pen and paper and center yourself with five deep breaths.
- Think about the days to come. Consider your priorities, remembering that every task is significant and an opportunity for increased mindfulness
- Ask yourself, "Am I giving myself adequate time to bring mindfulness and intentionality into each of these activities?"
- Take notice of any activities you feel you won't be able to be fully present for. Consider taking a thing or two off the list and saving them for a better time.
- Take notice of any feelings of stress, nervousness, or rush you feel in regards to your schedule. Breathe into those feelings.

- As you continue to write your schedule, allow yourself to feel empowered, in control, and prepared to be mindful of everything you are about to do

Mindful Driving

- Leave the house with plenty of time to be relaxed and focused. After entering the car, take a few moments to breathe and center yourself
- Once you start to drive, begin to take note of the things passing by. What do you see today that you did not see yesterday?
- Breathe in your visual surroundings, using them to center and remind yourself: "I am here. I am in this community. This is my life, and I am awake to it."

Mindful Walking (10-20-minute meditation)

- Choose an area where you can relax and bring attention to your surroundings. This can be in a park, in the city, on the beach, in your neighborhood, etc.
- Set out on your walk with no distractions
- Take notice of the things your eyes fall upon. If something specific catches your attention, allow yourself to pause and breathe it in.
- Pay attention to the sounds that surround you, giving yourself space to truly hear them

- Pay attention to the feeling of your feet on the pavement, the swing of your arms at your sides, and the rhythm of your breath
- Let your heart expand in curiosity and openness to whatever is ready to meet you in this space
- Allow yourself to become totally saturated with your surroundings, remembering that everything you see, hear, and feel is a part of you

Mindful Cooking and Eating

- As you enter the kitchen to prepare food, take a moment to center yourself in the moment with a few deep breaths
- Give every moment of the cooking process your full attention, from washing, to cutting, to cooking. Become fully immersed in the process (you can do this even with simple meals, like mindfully spreading peanut butter on bread)
- Breathe loving-kindness into the cooking process, remembering that the food you make will provide nourishment to yourself and others
- Once the food is ready, clear the eating space of distractions. Avoid multi-tasking
- Chew every bite of food 20-30 times, letting yourself be engulfed in the flavor and practicing gratitude for the nourishment
- Walk away from your meal feeling truly nourished and renewed

Mindful Waiting

- The next time you're trying to distract yourself at the doctor's office, the mechanic, or waiting for a friend or colleague to arrive, remind yourself that waiting is one of the most sacred times to engage in mindfulness

- Breathe into the moment, becoming aware of what surrounds you

- Bring awareness to your body. How are you feeling? Take note of any sensations

- Become aware of the thoughts that come once you stop numbing yourself with distractions. What things are running through your mind?

- Pay attention to the deeper thoughts you may have previously been ignoring. Ask yourself what you can learn about yourself and your life, or if there are any actions you need to take.

Mindful Creativity (at least 5 minutes)

- Set aside anywhere from five minutes to several hours of undivided time

- Engage in a creative project like art, writing, dancing, etc.

- Bring full presence to the creative project and try to eliminate all expectations. Allow the moment to carry you.

- Pay attention to how your mind and body react as the moment carries you. How do you feel?

- Examine what you create as a result of this free-flowing creativity

Mindful Play

- Dedicate time each week to doing something truly fun—something that makes you feel like a kid again (climbing a tree, swimming in the lake, drawing with chalk, baking cookies, having a game night, etc.)

- Eliminate all distractions and allow this to be a moment to step away from your everyday life and responsibilities

- Allow yourself to become lost in the childlike joy of play. Laugh loudly, let your body dance, be curious.

- Let the feeling of childlike joy saturate your body and carry this joy with you as you move back into your daily life.

Mindful Movement (10-30 minutes)

- Choose one of your favorite forms of movement (swimming, walking, dancing, going to the gym, etc.) and dedicate at least ten minutes to it

- As you begin to move, establish a deeper sense of body awareness. Pay attention to the feelings in your body as you begin to warm up and exercise

- Pay attention to the way your heart beats, your lungs heave, your face begins to sweat, and your body tingles with the sense of being alive

- Thank your body for all it does for you.

Mindful Listening/Quality Time

- Apply this meditation to any quality time you spend with another person, whether that is grabbing coffee or going for a walk with a loved one, interacting with co-workers, are conversing with the grocery store cashier

- Before interacting with others, bring attention to your levels of empathy. Set the intention to hold space for other people and the moments you share with them

- Eliminate distractions (like technology) and allow yourself to put everything else going on in your life on pause in order to be fully present

- One of the best ways to show love for people and to cultivate personal mindfulness is through mindful listening. Focus all of your attention on the other person and what they are saying. When you ask how their day is going, be present to hear the answer.

- Do not think of what your next move will be, what you will say, or where you will go. Simply be there, showing loving-kindness, holding space, and taking it all in.

Mini Meditation Toolbox: 10 Quick and Easy Meditations to Ease Stress, Depression, Addiction, Anxiety, Pain, Distraction, and Loss Using Mindfulness

Journaling the Consciousness (10-minute meditation)

- Sit down with a journal and a pen and set your timer for 10 minutes
- As thoughts, worries, or emotions arise, immediately write them down. Do not worry about structure, grammar, or content, just write.
- When the time is up, look over what you wrote
- Ask yourself which themes seem to reoccur. Where are you feeling stress in your life? What is occupying most of your mental space?
- Close your eyes and take a few moments to breathe and meditate on the thing(s) that need your attention the most
- Open your eyes. Notice how you feel lighter and in touch with your experience

Distraction Cleanse: Clearing the Space in your Mind

- *Find a quiet place and begin to breathe*
- Ask yourself: "What is distracting me from being present right now?"
- Give space to that distraction, whether it is an invasive thought, personal emotion, or someone else's emotion

- Say to yourself: "I am letting my distractions move through me as I ground myself in the present moment. Nothing is more important than right now."

- Breathe until you feel the distraction melt away into presence and mental clarity.

Re-Writing the Moment: A Short Meditation to Ease Emotional Pain of the Past

- Sit down with a journal and a pen and set your timer for 1 minute

- Take this 1 minute to write down any moment(s) of the past which have caused you a lot of pain

- After the minute is up, choose one of the painful moments, close your eyes, and begin to imagine the moment in a safe way. Be sure to keep breathing.

- When you open your eyes, take your pen and paper and re-imagine the painful moment. What do you wish had happened? How do you wish you could think about the moment now?

- After re-imagining the painful moment, remind yourself that this is a new moment. Everyone has painful memories, but you do not have to stay in spaces of the past, which are painful for you.

- Close your eyes, take a few more breaths, and say to yourself, "I release the pain of that moment of the past. This is a new moment, and I will move with it."

Re-claiming your Inner Power: A Short Meditation to Face Addiction

- Breathe into the moment, allowing yourself to think about the implications your addiction has on your life
- Without judgment, question your addiction. Ask yourself, "What has been left empty in me that I am trying to fill with this?" Listen for any emotions or past experiences of trauma, grief, or abandonment that arise. Allow them to be there.
- Say to yourself, "Now that I understand the root of my addiction, I can begin to be set free."
- With closed eyes, begin to breathe. With each breath, imagine your addiction's hold on you weakening and weakening until eventually, you have been released.
- Move forward into your life with the idea that your addiction's hold on you is loosening, day by day.

Letter to the Lost: A Short Meditation to Address Grief and Loss

- Sit down with a journal and a pen and take five deep breaths to bring you into the moment
- Allow someone you have lost to come to mind. This can be a relationship that has ended, someone who has died, etc.
- Close your eyes and breathe into the space this person has left empty within you. Allow yourself to experience any emotions that arise.
- When you open your eyes, take a few minutes to write what you wish you could have said to that person

- After you have finished your letter, close your eyes again. Tell your grief that it is okay for it to be there. With every breath, imagine yourself moving forward in your life, released from every regret you may have with someone you've lost

In with The Positive, Out with the Negative: A Short Breathing Technique

- Find a comfortable space and prepare to use the 5-5-7 breathing technique
- Breathe in for five counts and think of something positive you want to bring into this moment (kindness, peace, wisdom, etc.)
- Hold for five counts, allowing this positive thing to fill your body
- Exhale for seven counts, thinking of something negative you want to release from your body in this moment (stress, tension, selfishness, etc.)
- Begin again with a second emotion. Do this as many times as you like until you feel well-equipped with positive emotions and have released all negative ones

Space to Breathe: A Short Meditation to Gain Control over your Anxiety

- When you begin to feel anxious, step away, take a breath, and ground yourself in the moment by finding one thing you can see, one thing you can hear, and one thing you can feel. Focus deeply on each thing.

- Allow your anxiety space to exist. Remember, anxiety is the reaction your emotional brain has when it senses a threat. You can bring yourself back from catastrophe mode by using the rational brain to repeatedly remind yourself: "I am safe. I am in control. I am capable of being calm."
- Keep breathing and saying these rational-brained affirmations until you begin to feel your anxiety melt away
- Move into the next moment feeling calm, anxiety-free, and empowered

Emotion Coding: A Short Meditation to Bring you in Touch with your Emotions

- Find a quiet, comfortable place where you can easily connect with yourself
- Close your eyes and breathe deeply (you may use a breathing pattern if desired)
- Begin to travel inwards. Say to yourself, "I am ready to accept the emotions that are here."
- Wait patiently, focusing on the breath, and observing every emotion that rises to the surface.
- When an emotion arises, ask yourself a series of questions:

    1. "Is this emotion mine or someone else's?"
    2. "Does this emotion serve me or hold me back?"
    3. "What is this emotion trying to teach me?"
    4. "Should I release this emotion or put it into action?"

- When it comes to answering each question, listen to your intuition. The answers to each question are already within you. Do not question your natural answers.

- If you are being told to release an old or negative emotion, or an emotion that belongs to someone else, breathe and imagine it melting away with every exhale

- If you are being told to foster a positive emotion or a strong emotion that can create positive change in the world, sit with that, breathing, and being open to how that emotion can be useful.

The "I Love..." Gratitude Meditation (2-minute meditation)

- Find a private space, preferably one in front of a mirror

- Start a timer for 2 minutes

- For two minutes, speak out loud sentences of gratitude beginning with the words "I love…" ("I love my partner," "I love coffee," "I love my cat," "I love sunflowers," I love my mom," "I love to dance," "I love that I am healthy,").

- Say as many things as you can, one after the other. Do not think too much, simply let the things you love flow from your lips

- When the timer goes off, look in the mirror and say "And I love you," to yourself

- Feel the magic of gratitude transforming your life, your self-confidence, and your ability to be mindful

The Mindful Manifestation: A Short Meditation to Manifest what you Want in Life

- Sit down with a journal and pen

- Begin to cultivate mindfulness by bringing attention to your breath and any sensations in your body

- Ask yourself the question: "What do I want most in life?"

- As the answers start to come, open your eyes and begin to write your desires with the words "I manifest…" in front of them ("I manifest empathy." "I manifest peace of mind." "I manifest protection." "I manifest safety." "I manifest love." "I manifest awareness." "I manifest wisdom." "I manifest pure joy.")

- With each manifestation, close your eyes, and say it to yourself at least three times. Feel this manifestation become a part of your reality.

PART V

Chapter 1: Self-Care Is the Best Care

"It is so important to take time for yourself and find clarity. The most important relationship is the one you have with yourself."

-Diane Von Furstenberg

Self-care is any activity that we deliberately do to improve our own well-being, whether it is physical, emotional, mental, or spiritual. The importance of taking care of one's self cannot be denied, as even health care training focuses on making sure healthcare workers are caring for themselves. If you do not take care of yourself, eventually, every other aspect o your life will fall apart, including your ability to help others.

This is a very simple concept, yet it is highly overlooked in the grand scheme of things. People lack the tendency to look after themselves and put their needs before anyone else. Good self-care is essential to improving our mood and reducing our anxiety levels. It will do wonders for reducing exhaustion and burnout, which is very common in our fast-paced world. It will also lead to positive improvements in our relationships.

One thing to note is that self-care does not mean forcing ourselves to do something we don't like, no matter how enjoyable it is to other people. For example, if your friends are forcing you to go to a party you rather not attend, then giving in is not taking care of yourself. If you would rather stay in and watch a movie, then that's what you should do, and it will be better for your well-being.

How Does Self-Care Work

It is difficult to pinpoint exactly what self-care is, as it is personal for everybody. Some people love to pamper themselves by going to the spa, while others enjoy physical activities like hiking, biking, or swimming. Some individuals take up art or other hobbies, like writing or playing a musical instrument. These activities are all different but will have the same type of benefits for the individuals engaging in them.

The main factor to consider when engaging in self-care is to determine if you enjoy the activity in question. If not, then it's time to move on. Self-care is an active choice that you actually have to plan out. It is time you set aside for yourself to make sure all of your needs are met. If you use a planner of any sort, make sure to dedicate some space for your particular self-care activities. Also, let people who need to know about your plans so you can become more committed. Pay special attention to how you feel afterward. The objective of any self-care activity is to make yourself feel better. If this is not happening, then it's time to change the activity.

While self-care, as a whole, is individualized, there is a basic checklist to consider.

- Create a list of things you absolutely don't want to do during the self-care process. For instance, not checking emails, not answering the phone, avoiding activities you don't enjoy, or not going to specific gatherings, like a house party.

- Eat nutritious and healthy meals most of the time, while indulging once in a while.

- Get the proper amount of sleep according to your needs.

- Avoid too many negative things, like news or social media.

- Exercise regularly.

- Spend appropriate time with your loved ones. These are the people you genuinely enjoy and not forced relationships.

- Look for opportunities to enjoy yourself and laugh.

- Do at least one relaxing activity a day, like taking a bath, going for a walk, or cooking a meal.

Self-care is extremely important and should not be an anomaly in your life.

How Does Self-Care Improve Self-Esteem and Self-Confidence?

To bring everything full circle, self-care plays a major role in improving self-esteem and self-confidence. It is easy to see how taking care of yourself will also make you feel better about yourself overall. All of these are actually inter-related, and a lack of one showcases a lack of the other. While caring for yourself also improves your self-esteem and self-confidence, not having self-esteem or self-confidence also leads to a lack of self-care. Basically, you believe that you are not good enough to be taken care of.

People with high self-esteem and self-confidence value themselves as much as they value others, and have no issues with making sure they're taken care of. They realize that it does not make them selfish or inconsiderate to think in this manner. Even if other people try to make them feel that way, a self-confident person will just brush off the criticism. An important thing to note is that when you take care of yourself, it does not mean you don't care about other people. It simply means you have enough self-love to not place yourself on the backburner.

Many people work so hard to try and please everyone else. This is one of the telltale signs of low self-esteem. While they're busy worried about other peoples' needs, their own get neglected, which will wear them down over time. The more they're unable to please someone, the harder they will try. What people in this situation don't realize is that some people are impossible to please, and it is not their responsibility to please them. That is up to the individual.

Poor self-care will eventually lead to poor self-image. It is possible that a person already has this initially. Self-care includes taking care of your hygienic and grooming needs. If you don't take the time to make yourself look good, this will significantly impact the value you place on yourself. When you are t work, among your friends, or just walking around town, not feeling like you look good will ultimately make you feel like you don't belong anywhere. Your confidence levels will plummet due to this.

Your health is another aspect to consider. Poor self-care means bad sleeping habits, unhealthy diets, lack of exercise, and more self-destructive behaviors. Your poor health practices can result in chronic illnesses down the line, like heart disease or diabetes. Once again, diminished health will lead to reduced self-confidence and self-esteem. Ask yourself now if putting other people ahead of you is worth it? I've got some news for you. The people who demand the most from you are probably looking out for themselves first.

The less a person takes care of themselves, the more their self-esteem and self-confidence will decline. It turns into a vicious downward cycle. This is why it is important to focus on all of these areas equally. When you find yourself neglecting your own self-care practices, it is time to shift your direction and bring your attention back to your needs. Ignoring your needs will ultimately lead to your fall. We will discuss specific practices and techniques for improving self-care in the next chapter.

Chapter 2:

What Does Good Self-Care Look Like?

Good Self-Care Practices

The following are some ways that good self-care will look like. If you find yourself having these qualities, then you are on the right path.

Taking Responsibility for Your Happiness

When you engage in self-care, it is truly self-care. This means you only rely on yourself, and nobody else, to make sure your needs are met. You realize that your happiness is no one else's responsibility but your own. You alone have the ability to control your outcomes. As a result of this independence, you will develop the skills and attitude you need to care for your own physical, mental, emotional, and spiritual well-being.

You Become Assertive With Others

People often take assertiveness for rudeness. This is not true, but if people believe that standing firm for what you want is rude, then that's their problem. Once you reach a certain mindset where self-care is important to you, then you will be unapologetically assertive. This means you have the ability to say "no" with confidence and stand by it. "No" is a complete sentence, and people will realize that quickly when they hear it from you.

You Treat Yourself As You Would a Close Friend

It's interesting how we believe that other people deserve better treatment from us than we do ourselves. We have a tendency to put our best friends in front of us, no matter how detrimental it is to our lives. This behavior stops once we engage in proper self-care. At this point, you will treat yourself as good as, or even better, than you treat your most beloved friends.

You Are Not Afraid to Ask for What You Want

Once you learn to take care of yourself, you also see your value increase within your mind. This means having an understanding that your voice, opinion, and needs matter, just like anybody with high self-esteem and self-confidence, would. As a result, you will not be afraid to ask for what you want, even if you might not get it.

Your Life Is Set Around Your Own Values

Once you practice self-care, you learn to check in with yourself before making important decisions. You always make sure the choices you are about to make line up with your purpose and values. If they go against them, then it's not a path you choose. This goes for the career you choose, where you decide to live, and the relationships you maintain in your life.

While all of the traits are focused on self, but it will lead to better relationships with other people too. When you practice self-care, you are in a better state in every aspect of your being. This gives you the ability to take care of and help those you need you, as well. Self-care is not an option, but a necessity, and it must never be ignored. Taking care of yourself is not selfish, no matter what anybody tells you. If someone tries to make you feel guilty over this matter, then consider distancing or removing them from your life. You are not obligated to maintain relationships with people.

Chapter 3: Demanding Your Own Self-Care

We went over the importance of self-care, and now we will focus on making it a reality in your life. If you want self-care to occur, you must be willing to demand it. The world is full of people who expect you to be at there beck-and-call every moment of the day. Some of these individuals are those who are closest to us, like friends or family members. This can make it harder to make our demands heard, but there is no way around it. Taking care of yourself is not an idea you can budge on. It is extremely important. We will go over several ways to maintain your ability for self-care in your life and provide detailed action steps to help you progress in this area.

Setting Healthy Boundaries

One of the biggest obstacles to self-care is other people who surround you. These are the true selfish individuals, whether they realize it or not, who believe they can barge in on your life and deserve all of your attention. They will take advantage of you, and if you are not careful, they will completely gain control of your emotions, and even your life. For proper self-care to occur, you must set firm and healthy boundaries with people. The following are steps that need to become mainstays in your life.

Identify and Name Your Limits

You must understand what your emotional, physical, mental, and spiritual limits are. If you do not know, then you will never be able to set real boundaries with people. Determine what behaviors you can tolerate and accept, and then consider what makes you feel uncomfortable. Identifying and separating these traits will help us determine our lines.

Stay Tuned Into Your Feelings

Two major emotions that are red flags that indicate a person is crossing a barrier are resentment or discomfort. Whenever you are having these feelings, it is important to determine why. Resentment generally comes from people taking advantage of us or feelings of being unappreciated. In this instance, we are likely pushing ourselves beyond our limits because we feel guilty. Guilt-trips is a weapon that many people use to get their way. It is important to recognize when someone is trying to make you feel guilty because they are way overstepping their boundaries. Resentment could also be due to someone imposing their own views or values onto us. When someone makes you feel uncomfortable, that is another indication of a boundary crossed. Stay in tune with both of these emotions.

Don't Be Afraid of Being Direct

With some people, setting boundaries is easy because they have a similar communication style. They can simply read your cues and back off when needed. For other individuals, a more direct approach is needed. Some people just don't get the hint that they've crossed a line. You must communicate to them in a firm way that they have crossed your limits, and you need some space. A respectful person will honor your wishes without hesitation. If they don't, then that's on them. Your personal space is more important than their feelings.

Give Yourself Permission to Set Boundaries

The potential downfalls to personal limits are fear, self-doubt, and guilt. We may fear the other person's response when we set strong boundaries. Also, we may feel guilty if they become emotional about it. We may even have self-doubt on whether we can maintain these limits in the long run. Many individuals have the mindset that in order to be a good daughter, son, parent, or friend, etc., we have to say "yes" all the time. They often wonder if they deserve to have boundaries and limits with those closest to them. The answer is, yes, you do. You need to give yourself permission to set limits with people because they are essential to maintaining healthy relationships too. Boundaries are also a sign of self-respect. Never feel bad for respecting yourself.

Consider Your Past and Present

Determine what roles you have played throughout your life in the various relationships you have had. Were you the one who was always the caretaker? If so, then your natural tendency may be to put others before yourself. Also, think about your relationships now. Are you the one always taking care of things, or is it a reciprocal relationship? For example, are you always the one making plans, buying gifts, having dinner parties, and being responsible for all of the important aspects of the relationships? If this is the case, then tuning into your needs is especially important here. If you are okay with the dynamics of the relationship, then that's fine. I can't tell you how to feel. However, if you feel anger and resentment over this, then it's time to let your feeling be known, unapologetically.

Be Assertive

Once again, this does not mean being rude, even though some people will interpret it that way. Being assertive simply means being firm, which is important when reminding someone about your boundaries. Creating boundaries alone is not enough. You also have to stand by them and let people know immediately if they've crossed them. Let the person know in a respectful but strong tone that you are uncomfortable with where they're going, and they need to give you some space. Assertive communication is a necessity.

Start Small

Setting boundaries is a skill that takes a while to develop, especially if it's something you've never done before. Therefore, start with a small boundary, like no phone calls after a certain time at night. Make sure to follow through;

otherwise, the boundary is worthless. From here, make larger boundaries based on your comfort level.

Eliminating Toxicity and Not Caring About Losing Friends

If you plan on making self-care a priority in your life, I think that's great, and so should you. However, some people will have a problem with this. People don't always like it when their friends, family members, or acquaintances, etc., put themselves at the forefront of their lives. Once again, that is their problem, not yours. What is your problem, though, is distancing or even eliminating these individuals from your life. We will go over that in this section because part of self-care is eliminating toxicity from your life and not feeling bad about it.

Don't Expect People to Change

While everyone deserves a chance to redeem themselves, there comes the point where we must accept that people cannot change by force. They have to find it within themselves to make this change, and it is not our responsibility to do so. You may yearn to be the one who changes them, but it's usually a hopeless project. Toxic individuals are motivated by their problems. They use them to get the attention they need. Stop being the one to give it to them.

Establish and Maintain Boundaries

I already went in-depth on this, so I won't revisit it too much here. Just know that toxic people will push you to work harder and harder for them, while you completely ignore your own needs. This is exhausting and unacceptable. Create the boundaries you need with these individuals based on your own limits.

Don't Keep Falling for Crisis Situations

Toxic people will make you feel like they need you always because they are constantly in a crisis situation of some sort. It is a neverending cycle. When a person is in a perpetual crisis, it is of their own doing. They often create drama purposely to get extra attention. You may feel guilty for ignoring them, but remember that their being manipulative and not totally genuine.

I am not saying that you can't ever help someone who is going through a hard time. Of course, you can. Just don't start believing that you're responsible for their success or failure.

Focus on the Solution

Toxic individuals will give you a lot to be angry and sad about. If you focus on this, then you will just become miserable. You must focus on the solution, which, in this case, is removing drama and toxicity from your life. Recognize the fact that you will have less emotional stress once you remove this person from your life. If you let them, they will suck away all of your energy.

Accept Your Own Difficulties and Weaknesses

A toxic person will know how to exploit your weaknesses and use them against you. For example, if you are easy to guilt-trip, they will have you feel guilty every time you pull away from them. If you get to know yourself better and recognize these weaknesses, then you can better manage them and protect yourself. This goes along with creating self-awareness, which we discussed in chapter two. When you accept your weaknesses, you can work on fixing them and balance them with your strengths.

They Won't Go Easily

Recognize that a toxic individual may resist being removed from your life. Actually, if they don't resist, I will be pleasantly surprised. They may throw tantrums, but this is because they can't control or manipulate you anymore. They will even increase their previous tactics with more intensity. It is a trap, and you must not fall for it. Stay firm in your desire to leave and keep pushing forward. If they suck you back in, good luck trying to get out again.

Choose Your Battles Carefully

Fighting with a toxic person is exhausting and usually not worth it. You do not need to engage in every battle with them. They are just trying to instigate you.

Surround Yourself With Healthy relationships

Once you have removed a toxic person, or persons, from your life, then avoid falling into the trap with someone else. Fill your circle with happy and healthy relationships, so there is no room for any toxicity. Always remember the signs of a toxic person, so you can avoid them wholeheartedly in the future.

How to Focus on Self-Care

Now that we have worked to set boundaries and eliminate toxic people from our lives, it is time to focus on ourselves and the self-care we provide. The following are some self-care tips, according to psychologist, Dr. Tchiki Davis, Ph.D.

Pay Attention to Your Sleep

Sleep is an essential part of taking care of yourself. You must make it part of your routine because it will play a huge role in your emotional and physical well-being. There are many things that can wreak havoc on your sleep patterns, like stress, poor diet, watching television, or looking at your phone as you're trying to fall asleep. Think about your night routine. Are you eating right before bed or taking in a lot of sugar and caffeine? Are you working nonstop right up until bedtime? Have you given yourself some time to wind down before going to sleep? All of these factors are important to consider, as they will affect your sleep patterns. If you can, put away any phones, tablets, and turn off the television at least 30 minutes before you plan on going to bed.

Take Care of Your Gut

We often neglect our digestive tract, but it plays a major role in our health and overall well-being. When our gut is not working well, it makes us feel sluggish, bloated, and nonproductive. Pay attention to the food you eat as it will determine the health of your gut. It is best to avoid food with excess salt, sugar, cholesterol, or unhealthy fats. Stick to foods that are high in fiber, protein, healthy fats, and complex carbs. Some good options are whole grains, nuts, lean meats, fruits and vegetables, beans, and fish.

Exercise and Physical Activity Is Essential

Regular exercise is great for both physical and mental health. The physical benefits are obvious. However, many people do not realize that exercise will help the body release certain hormones like endorphins and serotonin. These are often called feel-good hormones because they play a major role in affecting our mood in a positive way. The release of these hormones will give us energy too, which will make us want to exercise more. Once exercise becomes a habit, it will be hard to break. Decide for yourself what your exercise routine will be, whether it's going to the gym, walking around the neighborhood, or playing a game of tennis.

Consider a Mediterranean Diet

While this is not a dietary book, the Mediterranean diet is considered the healthiest diet in the world because of its extreme health benefits. The food groups and ingredients that are used will increase energy, brain function, and has amazing benefits like heart and digestive tract health. The food also does not lack flavor, which shatters the myth that healthy food does not taste good.

Take a Self-Care Trip

Even if you are not much of a traveler, getting away once in a while can do wonders for your mental health. So often, our environment will make us feel stressed out, and it's good to remove ourselves from it for a couple of days. You do not have to take a trip abroad here. Of course, that is certainly an option. A simple weekend trip is perfectly fine. Just get yourself out of your normal routine and be by yourself for a while.

Get Outside

Nature and sunlight can be great medicines. It can help you reduce stress or worry, and has many great health benefits. Doing some physical activity outside, like hiking or gardening, are also great options.

Bring a Pet Into Your Life

Pets can bring you a lot of joy, and the responsibility they come with can boost your self-confidence by having to care for another living creature. Dogs are especially great at helping to reduce stress and anxiety. Animal therapy has been used to help people suffering from disorders lie PTSD, as well.

Get Yourself Organized

Organizing your life and doing some decluttering can do wonders for your mental and emotional health. Decide what area of your life needs to be organized. Do you need to clear your desk, clean out the fridge, or declutter your closet? Do you need to get a calendar or planner and schedule your life better? Whatever you can do to get yourself more organized, do it. Being organized allows you to know how to take better care of yourself.

Cook Yourself Meals At Home

People often neglect the benefits of a good home-cooked meal. They opt, instead, for fast-food or microwave dinners. These types of meals will make you full but will lack in essential nutrients that your body needs. Cooking nutritious meals at home will allow you to use the correct ingredients, so you can feel full and satisfied. Cooking alone can also be great therapy for people.

Read Regularly

Self-help books are a great read. However, do not limit yourself to these. You can also read books on subjects that you find fascinating or books that simply provide entertainment.

Schedule Your Self-Care Time

Just like you would write down an appointment time in your planner, also block out specific times for self-care activities. Stick to this schedule religiously, unless a true emergency comes up. This means that if a friend calls you to go out, you should respectfully decline their request and focus on yourself.

Chapter 4: How to Be Happy Being Alone

The final section of this book will focus on being alone and how to be happy about it. When you start engaging in self-care, you will also be spending much more time by yourself. A lot of people have a hard time dealing with this concept, especially if they're used to being around people all the time. However, for proper self-care, you have to be okay with being alone once in a while.

Accept Some Alone Time

The following are some tips to help you become happy with being alone. Soon, you will realize that your own company is the best kind.

Do Not Compare Yourself to Others

We are referring to your social life here. Do not compare to others, and do not feel like you must live as others do. If you do this, you may become jealous of a person's social circle or lifestyle. It is better to focus on yourself and what makes you happy. If you plan on spending significant time alone, then you cannot pay attention to what other people are doing.

Step Away From Social Media

If strolling through your social media page makes you feel left out, then take a step back and put it away for a while. During self-care moments, you are the focus, not what is happening with others online. Also, what people post on their pages is not always true. Many individuals have been known to exaggerate, or even flat-out lie on social media platforms. You may be feeling jealous or left out for no reason. Try banning yourself from social media for 24-48 hours, and see how it makes you feel.

Take a Break From Your Phone

Avoid making or receiving calls. Let the important people in your life know that you will be away from your phone for a while, so they don't worry. When you are alone, really try to be alone.

Allow Time for Your Mind to Wander

If you feel unusual about doing nothing, it is probably because you have not allowed yourself to be in this position for a while. Carve out a small amount of time where you stay away from TV, music, the internet, and even books. Use this time to just sit quietly with your thoughts. Find a comfortable spot to sit or lie down, then just let your mind wander and see where it takes you. This may seem strange the first time, but with practice, you will get used to the new freedom.

Take Yourself on a Date

You don't need to be with someone else to enjoy a night out on the town. Take a self-date and enjoy your own company for a while. Go to a movie by yourself, stop by a nice restaurant, or just go do an activity you enjoy. If you are not used to hanging out alone, give it some time and you will become more comfortable with it. Take yourself on that solo date.

Exercise

We have mentioned exercise and physical activity a lot, but that's because it has so many great benefits related to self-care. Exercising will uplift your mood, and make it more enjoyable to be by yourself. Those feel-good hormones will provide a lot of benefits during these times.

Take Advantage of the Perks of Being Alone

Some people have spent so much time with other people that they've forgotten the perks of being alone. There are many to consider. First of all, you do not have to ask anyone's permission to do anything; you will have more personal space, can enjoy the activities you want to do, and don't have to worry about upsetting anyone. If you want, you can even have a solo dance party in your living room, Tom Cruise style. There are many advantages to being alone, so use them.

Find a Creative Outlet

It is beneficial to use some of your alone time to work on something creative. This can be painting, sculpting, music, writing, or any other creative endeavors. In fact, you can get out the watercolors and start fingerpainting. Creativity will bring a lot of joy into your life. It will make you happier about being alone.

Take Time to Self-Reflect

Being alone will give you the opportunity to self-reflect on your life. You won't care so much about being alone when you are coming up with important answers to your life.

Make Plans for Your Future

Planning out your life for five or ten years down the line will give you something important to do, and something to look forward to. Alone time is the perfect opportunity to determine these plans.

Make Plans for Solo Outings

Plan your solo outings based on what you like to do, whether it's a farmer's market, hiking, riding your bike, or going camping alone. Mak plans that will excite you, and you will be taking care of yourself while also being okay alone.

There are numerous topics that we went over in this chapter, but they all relate back to one theme: Self-care. Always remember that to take proper care of yourself, you must consider the following ideas:

- Setting Boundaries
- Avoiding and ridding yourself of toxic people
- Focus on yourself and your needs
- Be okay with being alone

Focus on these areas, and you will be demanding your own self-care without ever apologizing for it.

www.ingramcontent.com/pod-product-compliance
Lightning Source LLC
Chambersburg PA
CBHW060325030426
42336CB00011B/1202